Internationalisation of Universities and the National Language

DUISBURGER ARBEITEN ZUR SPRACH- UND KULTURWISSENSCHAFT

DUISBURG PAPERS ON RESEARCH IN LANGUAGE AND CULTURE

Herausgegeben von / edited by Frank Polzenhagen und / and Monika Reif
Begründet von / founded by Ulrich Ammon, René Dirven und / and Martin Pütz

BAND / VOLUME 126

Notes on the quality assurance and peer review of this publication

Prior to publication, the quality of the work published in this series is reviewed by one of the editors of the series.

Danny Pieters /
Thijs Keersmaekers (eds.)

Internationalisation of Universities and the National Language

Language Policy Interventions and Case Studies

PETER LANG

Bibliographic Information published by the Deutsche Nationalbibliothek
The Deutsche Nationalbibliothek lists this publication in the Deutsche Nationalbibliografie; detailed bibliographic data is available in the internet at http://dnb.d-nb.de.

Library of Congress Cataloging-in-Publication Data
A CIP catalog record for this book has been applied for at the Library of Congress

ISSN 0934-3709
ISBN 978-3-631-81686-8 (Print)
E-ISBN 978-3-631-82275-3 (E-PDF)
E-ISBN 978-3-631-82276-0 (EPUB)
E-ISBN 978-3-631-82277-7 (MOBI)
DOI 10.3726/b17283

Peter Lang – Berlin · Bern · Bruxelles · New York · Oxford · Warszawa · Wien

This publication has been peer reviewed.

www.peterlang.com

In memory of Ulrich Ammon

Table of Contents

About the Editors and Contributors

Editors

Danny Pieters was professor at Tilburg University (1986–1992), before becoming professor at KU Leuven's Faculty of Law in 1989, where he is the head of the Institute for Social Law since 2005. He is in charge of the Research Unit Europe and Social Security (RUESS) since 1993, and programme director of the Master in European Social Security since 1998. Professor Pieters was a member of the Belgian Federal Parliament from 1994 to 2003 and from 2010 to 2013 (first in the Chamber of Representatives, then in the Senate where he was president in 2010–11). From 2013 to 2017, he was vice rector for Humanities and Social Sciences as well as International Policy at KU Leuven.

Thijs Keersmaekers is staff member at KU Leuven's Institute for Social Law. He holds a degree in Linguistics and Literature. His current work focuses on language legislation in small states.

Contributors

Kai L. Chan is senior manager at a Dubai-based public policy advisory firm. Previously he was part of the senior management team of a Montreal-based technology company. Prior to that he was a special advisor to the UAE Government on matters of competitiveness and statistics, with a focus on the use of global performance indices to guide policy. He was also a distinguished fellow at the INSEAD Innovation & Policy Initiative during his original tenure in the UAE. Before moving to the Middle East, Dr. Chan worked at a consumer finance merchant banking firm in New York. Prior to that he worked in the Singapore office of a global management consulting firm with projects in Europe and East Asia. Dr. Chan holds a BSc in Economics & Mathematics from the University of Toronto, and an MA and PhD in Economics from Princeton University.

Manuel Célio Conceição is professor of Language Sciences. He was director of the Faculty of Human and Social Sciences at the University of the Algarve from 2016 to 2020 and pro rector of the university between 2010 and 2013. Professor Conceição is a long-time member of the European Language Council/*Conseil Européen pour les Langues*, where he is the *ex officio* president. One of his main interests there lies with the evaluation of linguistic policies of universities in Europe. Professor Conceição has directed or co-directed several international research projects, in particular in his fields of specialisation: multilingual terminology, language policies, quality assessment in language teaching, and intercultural communication. In 2013, he was admitted into the *Ordre des Arts et des Lettres* as *Chevalier* by the French government.

Hermann Giliomee was professor of Political Studies at the University of Cape Town. He has been a fellow at Yale University, the University of Cambridge and the Woodrow Wilson Centre for International Scholars in Washington. From 1995 to 1997, he was president of the South African Institute of Race Relations. He is currently extraordinary professor of History at Stellenbosch University. Professor Giliomee often writes about South African history and contemporary politics. Fifteen books have seen the light under his name, among others: *The Shaping of South African Society: From Apartheid to Nation-building* (1989, with Lawrence Schlemmer) and *The Awkward Embrace: One-Party Domination and Democracy* (1999, with Charles Simkins). His *The Afrikaners: Biography of a People* (2003, published in Afrikaans as *Die Afrikaners: 'n Biografie*) was listed in *The Economist* as one of their Books of the Year in 2003.

Frans Gregersen was professor of Danish language at the University of Copenhagen from 1996 until the end of 2018. From 2005 to 2015 he was the director of the Danish National Research Foundation Center of Excellence, LANCHART, focusing on sociolinguistic studies of language change in real time. He was the chairman and convener of the group of experts working on parallel language policies for the Nordic Council of Ministers (2014–17). Currently, he is active in a project on the history of Danish structuralism.

Monika Kalin Golob is professor of Slovenian Language and Stylistics at the University of Ljubljana's Faculty of Social Sciences. She studied Slovenian Language and Literature (as major) and Comparative Literature (as minor) at the university's Faculty of Arts. She was a postdoctoral fellow on invitation of the Bavarian Government in Munich, an invited professor at the Department of Czech language at Charles University, and invited professor at the Faculty of Arts at the University of Zagreb. Her research fields are language culture, stylistics of journalism, PR and advertising, language planning and language policy. She published over 300 articles, book chapters and books on these topics. She was vice dean for Study and Student Affairs (2005–11, 2015–17) and from 2017 she is dean of the Faculty of Social Sciences at the University of Ljubljana.

Birute Klaas-Lang is professor of Estonian as a Foreign Language at the University of Tartu and the head of the Department for Applied Linguistics. Her research centers on language contacts, areal linguistics, typology, and language policy and planning. She was vice rector of the University of Tartu from 2005 to 2010, and visiting professor of Estonian at the University of Helsinki from 2012 to 2016. Professor Klaas-Lang was the head of the Estonian Language Council from 2005 to 2016 and resumed these responsibilities from 2019. She is one of the authors of the Estonian Language Development Strategy 2004–10 and 2011–17.

Helle Metslang is professor of Modern Estonian of the University of Tartu and head of the Department of Estonian. She is also adjunct professor of the University of Helsinki and of the University of Oulu. She was professor of Estonian at Tallinn University (2000–06) and visiting professor of Estonian at the University of Helsinki (2004–07). Her research centers on morphosyntax, language variation, language typology, historical sociolinguistics, and language policy. Professor Metslang is Chair of the Mother Tongue Society and member of *Academia Europaea* and *AcademiaNet*. She is member of the Estonian Language Council and one of the authors of the Estonian Language Development Strategy 2004–10 and 2011–17.

Eric Mijts studied Linguistics and Literature at the University of Antwerp and is specialised in sociolinguistics. In 2000, he joined the University of Aruba where he works as a researcher and lecturer in skills and linguistics as well as an initiator of educational innovation and multidisciplinary and interdisciplinary research programmes. As a researcher he is affiliated with the University of Antwerp and Ghent University. He coordinates the Academic Foundation Year and the UAUCU student research exchange and he is a founding member of the SISSTEM programme (Sustainable Island Solutions through Science, Technology, Engineering and Mathematics). His research and publications focus on multilingualism, language policy and planning, education for sustainable development, and inclusion/exclusion processes.

Ivan Svetlik is professor of Human Resources and Social Policy at the University of Ljubljana. He was minister of Labour, Family and Social Affairs of Slovenia (2008–12) and was a member of the editorial committee of the *European Journal of Vocational Training* edited by CEDEFOP. In the period from 2013 to 2017, he was rector of the University of Ljubljana where he paid special attention to the internationalisation and language issues. Professor Svetlik has been involved in the country's labour market, social security, education and training reforms, and in consulting in these fields in the Balkan countries and in HRM in companies. His main research topics and interests are work, employment, education, human resources, social security, and quality of life. He published over 400 articles, book chapters and books on these topics.

Acknowledgements

We would like to thank all contributors to the symposium 'Internationalisation of Universities and the National Language' of 4 May 2018 at KU Leuven for making the event a great success and for sparking an interesting discussion on the need for language policies accompanying internationalisation strategies. We thank Karen M. Lauridsen for her expertise and Richard Wyn Jones for his passion on the subject. We thank Josep Soler for his help in outlining this volume. We thank all contributors of the present volume for their dedication to this publication. Without the help of all these people, today's volume wouldn't have been possible.

We also thank all people at KU Leuven who have made the conference and subsequent publication possible, with special thanks to Karine Op de Beeck for her preparatory work in outlining the symposium.

Finally, we thank Ulrich Ammon for his interesting contribution during the symposium, but also for introducing this work to the series *Duisburger Arbeiten zur Sprach- und Kulturwissenschaft*/Duisburg Papers on Research in Language and Culture. His unexpected passing means a great loss for the sociolinguistic community.

Leuven, February 2020

List of Abbreviations

ANC	African National Congress
CEFR	Common European Framework of Reference for Languages
CPUT	Cape Peninsula University of Technology
DHET	Department for Higher Education and Training
EAA	Estonian Academy of Arts
EAMT	Estonian Academy of Music and Theatre
EBS	Estonian Business School
EEIS	Estonian Educational Information System
EFNIL	European Federation of National Institutions for Language
EMI	English-Medium Instruction
EPI	English Proficiency Index
ERIS	Estonian Research Information System
EULS	Estonian University of Life Sciences
f.o.b.	free on board
FX	foreign exchange
GDP	gross domestic product
HAUs	Historically Afrikaans Universities
HE	higher education
HEI	higher education institutions
HELP	higher education language policy
HEMIS	Higher Education Management Information System
IB DP	International Baccalaureate diploma
IMF	International Monetary Fund
ISCED	International Standard Classification of Education
L1	first language
L2	second language
MENA	Middle East and North Africa
NP	National Party
NRF	National Research Foundation
NWU	North-West University
PLI	Power Language Index
PPP	purchasing power parity
PU	Potchefstroom University
RAU	Rand Afrikaans University
RU	Rhodes University
SAR	special administrative region
SDR	special drawing rights

SIDS	Small Island Developing States
SNO	supranational organisation
SU	Stellenbosch University
TalTech	Tallinn University of Technology
TU	Tallinn University
UCT	University of Cape Town
UFS	University of the Free State
UL	University of Ljubljana
UN	United Nations
UN	University of Natal
UOFS	University of the Orange Free State
UP	University of Pretoria
UT	University of Tartu
UWC	University of the Western Cape
WB	World Bank
Wits	University of Witwatersrand

List of Tables

Danny Pieters and Thijs Keersmaekers

Preface

In this introduction, the motivation behind the creation of the volume is explained. It serves as a first problem statement on the topic of language policy in higher education: how can we reconcile being international with protecting the national or local language? On top of that, the selection of contributions is justified.

In recent years, the growing interest among sociolinguists and language policy and planning scholars on the topic of the internationalisation of universities has generated a remarkable growth of publications in the form of edited collections and a myriad of journal articles touching upon the challenges and pressures on universities and their stakeholders in current times. What all these publications and many others invariably indicate, regardless of the angle of their approach, is that universities have become an interesting field for research on sociolinguistic and language policy aspects because of the opposed (sometimes indeed conflicting) sides that they embody: on the one hand, universities are seen by a range of stakeholders as key state institutions, one of whose main functions is connected with the protection, promotion, and development of national language(s) and culture(s); on the other hand, universities are also more and more pressed to become relevant international players within a global scene of international higher education, acting as key poles of attraction for researchers and students from all kinds of origins and backgrounds. Inevitably, then, this leads many universities to feel increasingly a kind of double bind, making efforts to maintain their national and local language(s) in this important domain of use while opening up room for other languages, most commonly English, to play an important role in their everyday landscape.

On 4 May 2018, experts in the field of language planning and language policy convened in Leuven to participate in a symposium focusing precisely on the issues described above, around the topic of the internationalisation of universities and the role of national language(s)[1]. How can we reconcile being international with protecting the national or local language? How can the global edge and the local function of universities be effectively combined? Those were some of the guiding questions that presenters and panellists touched upon throughout the day. Contributions ranged from analysing the status of English worldwide and its historical trajectory towards becoming a dominant language in higher education and academia, to case study presentations of university contexts from a wide range of settings, including European as well as African and Caribbean countries and regions.

There is a need to bring together studies encompassing these regional, national, and local perspectives in the frame of one coherent volume that can make the shared issues of universities in such different geographic and sociological contexts explicit, while at the same time highlighting peculiarities of each case in contrast to other cases. Therefore, this volume combines case-study contributions from countries and regions from within and outside Europe in order to underline the key language policy challenges facing universities around the world, in their attempt to remain nationally leading and internationally competitive institutions. The range of questions addressed by the authors in the volume include, but are not limited to, the following:

- What is the position of the national/local language in the specific country/region under study?
- What is the position of English and other international languages in the specific country/region under study?
- What explicit or implicit language policies exist that address the question of the internationalisation of higher education, both at the state and at the institutional levels?
- What major themes/discourses emanate from these policy documents (key goals, implementation strategies, agents involved, etc.)?

The volume starts by taking stock. The use of English as the *lingua franca* in international higher education and research is widespread, but exactly how influential is English compared to other languages? Kai L. Chan developed a system to measure the 'power' of a language, by looking at its impact according to several opportunities afforded by language: geography, economy, communication, knowledge & media, and diplomacy. Within each of these, Chan selected a set of variables that measure the effectiveness of language in capitalizing on these opportunities. While the dominance of English is undeniable, the study also makes a strong case for multilingualism.

Next, Manuel Célio Conceição looks at language policies in higher education and their inherent link with internationalisation. He stresses the rapid changes that have occurred in higher education due to globalisation, and their consequences for higher education institutions. While the language issue is absent in most internationalisation documents, Conceição claims that it should be a determining factor in internationalisation strategies. He argues that a higher education language policy (HELP) should foster multilingual competences to avoid education being reduced to monolingual practices.

The second part of the volume focuses on European case studies by looking at the language situation (specifically of universities) in Central Europe, the Baltic region, and the Nordic countries. Ivan Svetlik and Monika Kalin-Golob look at the case of Slovenia, focusing on the pressures of internationalisation for small nations. They scrutinize the policy documents that are in place on a national level before continuing to look at their implementation at the University of Ljubljana: how can a specific university find a balanced language policy in the process of internationalizing?

For the Baltic region, Birute Klaas-Lang and Helle Metslang present the case of Estonia. They describe the language situation in the country as well as at university, and study language policy strategies and the legal background of the national language. The main focus is on Estonian higher education and the impact of language policy strategies there, but the political debate concerning these strategies is considered as well. The chapter shows that while language policies are in place, increasing internationalisation efforts require a new balance in language use. However, the sustainability of Estonian is regaining its place as a developmental priority in the language debate.

Frans Gregersen takes a broader perspective of the Nordic countries and looks at policy initiatives encompassing the entire region. Gregersen investigates Nordic collaboration in the language domain and focuses on policy perspectives on language use. This provides an interesting background to look at language use at universities in the Nordic countries. Here, the focus is on the work of the Nordic Council of Ministers towards parallel language policies. The necessary indicators for a language policy are discussed, as well as best practices.

For the final part of the volume, we will look beyond Europe's borders and consider postcolonial states. These states are often prone to more complex language situations. Although English has become the dominant language worldwide, postcolonial states often also have to contend with the dominance of the former colonizer's language, to the detriment of the home language(s) of the population. Hermann Giliomee focuses on Afrikaans as a language of instruction in South African universities. While Afrikaans has quickly developed into a full-fledged scientific language, its use in higher education has also rapidly declined as the perceived language of apartheid.

Eric Mijts provides case studies of Aruba and Haiti. His focus is on postcolonial small island states. In many such states, the home language of the population has had to go through a long process to receive any form of recognition, if receiving recognition at all. Even once this recognition has been attained, the language of the former colonizer remains dominant, especially in higher education. Mijts claims that universities should take up a leading role in championing these home languages in order to emancipate the population.

The grouping of different countries and contexts leads to the scrutiny of a variety of scopes that complement each other. Which difficulties are there to overcome, which basis should be covered, and how do you demand space for yourself? All of this leads to specific and applicable policy suggestions at the end of the volume.

Note

1. See https://www.kuleuven.be/studiedag/50jaarleuvenvlaams-internationaal/english

Part I Background: Languages in the World and in Higher Education

Kai L. Chan

Power Language Index: The World's Most Powerful Languages

There are over 6,000 languages spoken in the world today, but some 2,000 of them count fewer than a thousand speakers. Moreover, just 15 of them account for half of the languages spoken in the world in terms of population. But which are the world's most influential languages? The Power Language Index (PLI) is a measure of a language's efficacy by measuring its influence in five domains ("opportunities"): geography, economy, communication, knowledge & media, and diplomacy. Altogether the PLI uses 20 (cardinal) indicators to arrive at an assessment of the power of over 100 languages. In this chapter, we will go over how the index was constructed, including the challenges of mapping data—almost invariably collected at the nation-state level—to languages, and the politics and other issues that make measuring the efficacy of languages difficult. However, no matter how the data are sliced and diced, the sheer influence of English is undeniable. Nevertheless, in spite of the fact that English is by far the most powerful language, the PLI also shows that true power comes to those who also possess a second (or third, or fourth …) language.

Keywords: languages, influence, English, multilingualism

Introduction

There are over 6,000 languages spoken in the world today, but some 2,000 of them count fewer than a thousand speakers. Moreover, the top 15 languages account for about half of the global population. The language that counts the highest number of native speakers is Mandarin Chinese, the official language of China (and Taiwan), at close to one billion. Spanish is the second most common mother tongue at close to half a billion. English places third with over 400 million native speakers—but it counts over 500 million second language speakers (and many more who speak a broken but passable variant of it), and is generally regarded as the global *lingua franca*. Rounding out the top five are Hindi and Arabic, both at around 300 million.

A pertinent question to ask is, which language is the most influential and important? Is the number of speakers the sole criterion? Obviously that should not be the case. Another important factor is the economic clout behind each language. Mandarin Chinese is the official language of China, a country that has recently overtaken the United States as the world's largest economy (when measured using purchasing power parity GDP (gross domestic product)). Geography is also relevant. Spanish is spoken in most of Latin America, French is spoken on three continents, and Russia is almost twice as large as the next nation. And language is essentially a means of acquiring and sharing knowledge, and a way of consuming media. Within media, an absolute majority of internet content is in English, while India is the world leader in the number of feature films produced. Language is also at the heart of diplomacy. Here, English is the working language of most international organisations; yet French has a standing on par with English, as it happens to be an official (although not the working) language of just as many major supranational institutions.

Hitherto most measures of the power of a language have been limited to simply examining the number of speakers of a language. In some cases the economic strength associated with languages is taken as the factor that languages derive their significance from. Some studies have tried to ascertain the influence or reach of languages by mapping their usage and footprint in social media and others. However, to tackle the question of which is the most powerful language requires a more holistic approach. Any such measure needs to simultaneously incorporate all of the factors above, as well as additional details in assessing the fortitude of languages.

In this chapter we will define a real-valued index to measure the 'power' of a language. We construe power as the ability of a language to help its user engage in the basic functions of language. Broadly speaking, there are five opportunities provided by language:

1. Geography: the ability to travel
2. Economy: the ability to participate in an economy
3. Communication: the ability to engage in dialogue
4. Knowledge and media: the ability to acquire and share information
5. Diplomacy: the ability to engage in international relations

The index should be neutral in that it should measure the usefulness of a language to a representative human being. It should not, a priori, apply to any particular person with his/her own set of conditions, preferences and geography. Indeed, the thought experiment is to imagine an alien landing on the Earth who wants to optimally interact with humans. Which language would afford this alien the best ability to interact with humans and succeed on this planet (the matter of the varying difficulties of learning different languages is set aside)?

To achieve the widest appeal, the index should be simple and intuitive, yet at the same time be a robust measure of the efficacy of languages. The chapter below describes the methodology chosen for the Power Language Index (PLI).

Methodology

The Power Language Index is a systematic way of evaluating the influence and reach of languages, using 20 indicators to measure five basic opportunities afforded by language: geography, economy, communication, knowledge & media, and diplomacy. For each of these, there is a set of variables to measure the effectiveness of language in capitalizing on the opportunity.

The index is constructed so that each of the first four opportunities are equally weighted at 22.5 % apiece of the final score. The final pillar thus constitutes 10.0 % of the index score. Each of the underlying indicators are cardinal measures of the reach of the language. Indicators were chosen based on their availability (either at the level of nations or languages), as well as their being a good proxy to measure efficacy of languages according to the five pillars of the index.

Based on these indicators the Power Language Index ranks the relative potency of 124 languages. The languages assessed through this index were chosen based on a multi-stage process. In the first stage, a list of languages was created: (1) a list of the top-100 languages by number of native speakers was compiled, (2) that list was augmented with languages covered by Google Translate, and (3) languages that are national languages of members of the United Nations (UN) states were added. In the second stage, languages were winnowed out according to the following criteria: (1) languages with less than one million native speakers were eliminated unless it is the national language of a UN member state and (2) languages which have insufficient data coverage were further sifted out.

Another challenge is classifying languages and distinguishing (in a consistent format) between a dialect and a language. It is said that the difference between a language and a dialect is that a language is a dialect with an army and a navy. As far as possible, languages are distinguished by linguistic (e.g. mutual intelligibility) rather than political factors in what follows. Nevertheless, there still remains a large grey zone in deciphering between the two. For example, Cantonese (and other variants of Chinese) is viewed by some as a dialect of Chinese while others classify it as a language. Often this distinction has much to do with politics. Likewise, Hindi and Urdu are the same languages in different scripts that have evolved and acquired their own unique features over time.

Unfortunately, data for the indicators are constructed under their own rules which need not align with how languages are dealt with according to the index. Notwithstanding the issue of how indicators map to languages or dialects, there is also the challenge of mapping data that are generated at the nation state level to the level of languages.

Matching data on the 20 variables to the 124 languages in the index is not straightforward, as most data are not tied directly to a language. Rather, the majority are linked with nation states, and often these entities have multiple languages associated with them. Furthermore, a language may have official status in a country but not be in effective use (e.g. Romansh in Switzerland). And languages might not be uniformly spread within a country (i.e. certain languages may be spoken only in specific geographic regions).

To derive the index score all the indicators are first mapped into the [0,1] interval by expressing them as a ratio of the maximum indicator value. They are then weighted and summed to derive the final index score.

Note that the index does not measure the beauty/merit of a language or its associated culture(s). Rather, it serves simply to show which languages are dominant in society and what doors are open to a speaker of a given language. Likewise, it is not a guide, per se, on which language(s) to learn as that is dependent on personal situation (including languages already known).

Grouping & Weights

Within each opportunity that language offers, the contribution of each indicator is inversely proportional to the number of indicators within that group. However, some indicators are assigned a half weight within their respective opportunity (denoted with an asterisk (*) in Table 1.1 below). This is done to take into account that some variables logically seem less relevant than their peers

Table 1.1: Overview of Indicators

GEOGRAPHY (22.5 %)	ECONOMY (22.5 %)	COMMUNICATION (22.5 %)	KNOWLEDGE&MEDIA (22.5 %)	DIPLOMACY (10.0 %)**
Countries spoken*	GDP (PPP)	Native speakers	Internet content	IMF
Land area	GDP/cap (PPP)*	L2 speakers*	Feature films*	UN
Tourists (inbound)*	Exports	Family size	Top-500 universities	WB
	FX market	Tourists (outbound)	Academic journals*	Index of 10 SNOs
	SDR composition			

* Half weight within its opportunity; indicator weights are otherwise distributed evenly within each opportunity.

** Indicator variables that take on value of 1 if an official/working language of the institution and 0 otherwise.

(within the same opportunity). For example, the number of native speakers has full weight while the number of second language speakers (L2) is assigned a half weight. Indicators in the diplomacy opportunity are indicator variables that take on a value of 1 when the condition is true and 0 otherwise. The indicators receive more attention in the section 'Indicators'.

Mapping

Many of the indicators used in the index are not directly linked with a language. Rather the bulk are associated with nation states/economies. To map indicator values associated with nation states to languages it is required to define within a country its dominant and minority languages. A 'dominant' language is one that is widely spoken and, for the most part, the majority mother tongue of a country. It is the (or a) *de facto* working language of a country and often has some form of official status. A 'minority' language, on the other hand, is one subordinate to the dominant language but still has a significant presence (minimum threshold of 10–15 % native speakers, but also dependent on its geographical concentration); it often also has some kind of official status or political recognition ("minority"). Having status as an official language of a country is neither necessary nor sufficient to be classified as either dominant or minority.

Then for each indicator associated with a nation-state, the value is mapped to its dominant language(s) by a factor of 1; for minority language(s) it is mapped by a factor of ½. For example, in Canada English is spoken by roughly ¾ of the population and is geographically widespread, whereas French is the mother tongue of about ¼ of the population and is spoken primarily in the provinces of Quebec. Both languages have official (and equal) status in Canada (at the federal level). Here English would take on a value of 1, while French would count as ½. So the full GDP of Canada is mapped to English, while French gets recognized for half that value.

The number of countries for which the indicators in the index are assessed are the 193 countries recognized by the UN, as well as a few large states outside of the UN charter (e.g. Kosovo and Taiwan) and exceptional cases (e.g. Hong Kong).

Missing Values

Where data are missing, the index takes the most conservative approach by assuming them to be zero. This is generally inconsequential as data which are missing are generally from sources where the likely true values are indeed zero or close to zero. Indeed, for the indicators in the index, missing data typically affect only the least developed countries which generally have no or low values for the associated variables. In exceptional cases the data may be estimated by interpolation or by econometric estimation. But generally, the index applies a strict approach to missing data, partly to encourage data reporting and as a means to avoid biasing the index by shifting the weights to included indicators, which in itself can lead to robustness failures.

Omitted Variables

The index strives to be parsimonious and the indicators included were specifically chosen to be cardinal variables (so that the index itself is a cardinal measure). For sure there are many indicators not included whose inclusion would help make the index more robust, for example, size and geographic reach of expat and diaspora communities etc. An obvious limitation is the availability of such data.

Transformation

All 20 of the indicators in the index are non-negative cardinal-valued variables. They are all 'positive' in that higher values are associated with more language efficacy. They are transformed to a score in the [0,1] range by dividing the raw indicator value by the maximum value in the sample: $s_i = x_i / x_{max}$ (so for each indicator there will be at least one language that takes on the maximal score of one).

Aggregation

The transformed scores of the 20 indicators are aggregated into an index score for a country by summing the weighted scores of the indicators: $I = \Sigma_j \omega_j s_j$. Since each transformed score takes a value in the range [0,1] it follows that the aggregated index score also falls in the range [0,1].

Note that the aggregated final index score is a cardinal measure. This is because all the inputs are themselves cardinal and transformed in a way that preserves cardinality.

Indicators[1]

Geography

Knowledge of a language enables the ability to travel and explore geography. This opportunity is divided in several indicators as listed below.

*Number of countries where language is spoken**. This indicator captures the number of countries in which a language is spoken—typically as a native tongue, but sometimes also as a second language. Note that the language spoken can be, and is often the case, highly different than the official language(s) of a country. For example, in some African nations French is the official language even though very few actually speak it as a mother tongue or at home. Nevertheless, in the case of many post-French-colonial African nations French acts as the effective *lingua franca* (typically spoken at L2 level) given the otherwise disparate and numerous varieties of indigenous languages. As per the mapping rule, if a language is deemed 'dominant' it counts as full, whereas if it is 'minority' it counts as half.

Data used for this indicator has been taken from the following sources: UN, national censuses (2016 or most recent).

Land area. The total land and inland water area within the recognized borders of a country, not including territorial claim on the seas. This indicator corrects for the fact that not all countries are equal in size. Knowledge of a language enables the exploration of a country. No adjustment is made on quality of land—every square kilometre of land is exactly interchangeable with any other in the world.

Data used for this indicator has been taken from the following sources: CIA Factbook, national sources (2016).

Tourists (inbound).* The number of international inbound tourists (overnight visitors) whose main purpose is other than business. This indicator captures the desirability of a given land and hence of its associated language(s). It partially corrects for the land area indicator as it, in a sense, is a proxy for the desirability of land.

Data used for this indicator has been taken from the following source: World Bank (WB, 2014 or most recent).

Economy

Language enables participation in the economic life of a country where it is spoken. However, when international business transactions are conducted they are often done in a third language. This opportunity is divided in several indicators as listed below.

GDP (PPP). Gross domestic product—i.e. the market value of goods and services produced within an economy in a given year—measured in purchasing power parity (PPP) international dollars. PPP is generally preferred to the nominal measure of GPD when making cross-country comparisons. Knowledge of a language enables one to participate in economies where that language is used.

Data used for this indicator has been taken from the following sources: International Monetary Fund (IMF), World Bank (2015 or most recent).

*GDP per capita (PPP)**. Gross domestic product—see above—measured in purchasing power parity international dollars divided by total population. Large countries might be on a whole rich, but poor on a per capita basis. GDP per capita is a proxy for the average standard of living in a country and thus also for the economic attractiveness of a country.
Data used for this indicator has been taken from the following sources: IMF, World Bank (2015 or most recent).

Exports. The US dollar (f.o.b.) value of goods sold by a country into foreign markets in a calendar year. Exports from a country are a means by which countries (and hence languages) exert their influence on the international stage. Importing nations receive both goods and soft culture (e.g. language) from their trading partners.
Data used for this indicator has been taken from the following source: CIA Factbook (2014 or most recent).

*Foreign exchange (FX) market**. The share of foreign exchange transactions (by value) in the global foreign exchange market. Note that the sum is 200 % because each trade is a two-way transaction. This indicator is a proxy for the global economic heft of countries, as expressed by the share of market turnover by currency in the foreign exchange market. Currencies are mapped to languages based on the 'presumed' home country of the currency. In some cases, a country might not have its own sovereign currency (e.g. dollarisation). In this case, English (in the case of dollarisation) is overrepresented.
Data used for this indicator has been taken from the following sources: Bank for International Settlements, Investopedia (2015).

*Special drawing rights (SDR) composition**. The foreign exchange assets maintained by the IMF. This indicator is a reflection of the global financial power structure. SDRs are pseudo-currencies of foreign exchange reserves managed by the IMF. It is the unit of account for the IMF. Its composition is based on four currencies as defined in Table 1.2.

Mapping the EUR to languages is based on the share of Eurozone GDP of the respective countries. Where multiple official (and *de facto*) languages of

Table 1.2: Weight of Currency by Language

CURRENCY	USD (USA)	EUR (Eurozone)	CNY (China)	JPY (Japan)	GBP (UK)
COMPOSITION	41.73 %	30.93 %	10.92 %	8.33 %	8.09 %
LANGUAGE	English	Various	Mandarin	Japanese	English

Source: Adapted from the IMF website and national censuses

communication exist in a single country, the GDP is split equally across the languages. This works as countries where this condition holds are generally split evenly in terms of population and economic size by language.
Data used for this indicator has been taken from the following sources: IMF, national censuses (2016).

Communication

Language is a means of interacting and communicating with others. The communication opportunity captures how language facilitates social interactions with other humans. This opportunity is divided in several indicators as listed below.

Native speakers. The total number of native speakers of a language. It may include people who are (fully) bilingual and thus may double count people across languages.
Data used for this indicator has been taken from the following sources: national censuses (most recent).

Second language (L2) speakers.* The total number of people who speak a language as a functional second language. This excludes, for example, students who (casually) study a language in an academic setting. It is primarily a measure of people who regularly communicate in a second language. For example, native Russian speakers who live in Ukraine and speak Ukrainian at a proficient level (typically in interacting with native Ukrainian speakers within their country).
Data used for this indicator has been taken from the following source: Ethnologue.

Family size.* The total number of native speakers from a given language family (e.g. Romance). It excludes, for a given language, its own count within its family in order to avoid double counting.

Knowledge of a particular language enables speakers to pick up the language of similar/related languages. For example, Italian and Spanish speakers are mostly able to understand each other (in spoken and written language) even without formal training in the other language. Likewise, a native Cantonese speaker (who is literate in Cantonese) is able to read a Mandarin-language newspaper (the (formal) written languages are nearly identical).

The family grouping is usually chosen at a level where there is some mutual intelligibility. Often this can be found two or three levels below the standard family grouping. For example, Polish belongs to the Indo-European family, which further branches out to Balto-Slavic, then Slavic, then West Slavic, then Lechitic, then Polish. For Polish, Slavic is considered the family.

This variable also takes into account cases where languages may share a common but unique script. For instance, many Chinese characters are used in Japanese (known as kanji). Because kanji is one of three script systems in the Japanese language, the Chinese language family is given a weight of just one third in Japanese (and vice versa).
Data used for this indicator has been taken from the following source: Ethnologue.

Knowledge & Media

One of the primary purposes of a language is to enable the consumption of media, and to acquire and share information. This opportunity is divided in several indicators as listed below.

Internet content. The share of internet sites and traffic displayed in a given language. Much of the media and knowledge (i.e. the stock of facts, information and skills of human development) we consume is on the internet. Although there are services that translate web content, the translations are often not great and web surfers seldom will browse sites in a language they do not know.
Data used for this indicator has been taken from the following source: W3Techs.com (2015).

Feature films.* The total number of feature films produced in a country. This can be seen as a reflection of the soft power of a language and the extent to which the language is consumed and shared as a medium of entertainment.
Data used for this indicator has been taken from the following source: Unesco Institute for Statistics (2014).

Top-500 universities. The number of top-500 universities as defined by ARWU (Shanghai JT University). Note that the language of instruction for a university does not necessarily correspond with the dominant, minority or official language of a country. This would tend to undercount the influence of English, which is sometimes the medium of instruction even in countries where it is not widely spoken.
Data used for this indicator has been taken from the following sources: Shanghai Jia Tong University, Academic Ranking of World Universities (2015).

Academic journals.* The number of peer-reviewed academic journals produced in a given language. There may be cases where a journal has more than one language of publication (e.g. some Canadian journals that are bilingual English-French) so the total count by languages may exceed the total population of journals.
Data used for this indicator has been taken from the following source: Wikipedia.

Diplomacy

The diplomacy opportunity reflects which languages are used in global settings at supranational organisations (SNOs). Most such institutions have a combination of official and working languages (i.e. languages for official communication and work). Many SNOs have multiple official languages but typically have a single *de facto* working language (almost always English). This opportunity is divided in several indicators as listed below.

IMF. This is an indicator variable that takes on the value '1' if a language is an official language of the International Monetary Fund or for which official communication is translated in a given language, and '0' otherwise. The IMF has seven official/working languages: English (official), Arabic, Chinese (Mandarin), French, Japanese, Russian and Spanish.

UN. This is an indicator variable that takes on the value '1' if a language is an official language of the United Nations and '0' otherwise. The UN has six official/working languages: Arabic, Chinese (Mandarin), English, French, Russian and Spanish.

World Bank. This is an indicator variable that takes on the value '1' if a language is an official language of the World Bank and '0' otherwise. The World Bank has six official/working languages: Arabic, Chinese (Mandarin), English, French, Russian and Spanish.

Index of 10 organisations. This is an index comprised of 10 indicator variables. Each of these takes on the value '1' if a language is an official/working language of the institution and '0' otherwise. The index is thus created by summing these values and dividing by the total number of institutions (10), thus creating an index indicator whose value ranges from 0 to 1. The 10 organisations in the index are:

1. Bureau International des Expositions (BIE)
2. Fédération Internationale de Football Association (FIFA)
3. International Criminal Court (ICC)
4. International Labour Organisation (ILO)
5. International Olympic Committee (IOC)
6. Inter-Parliamentary Union (IPU)
7. International Telecommunication Union (ITU)
8. Organisation for Economic Cooperation and Development (OECD)
9. Universal Postal Union (UPU)
10. World Trade Organisation (WTO)

Results

It should come as no surprise that English is (by far) the most powerful language with a score of 0.889. It is the *de facto* language of the largest (nominal GDP) economy (USA) and for two other G7 nations (UK and Canada). It is the global *lingua franca*. Mandarin comes second with a score of 0.411 on the strength of the Chinese economy and its sheer number of speakers. French (0.337) just edges Spanish (0.329), both of which have a far-reaching geographic coverage. Trailing are Arabic (0.273) and Russian (0.244), which are geographically concentrated but span large land areas. The top 6 languages—even if diplomacy is ignored—also happen to be the official languages of the United Nations. The remaining four in the top 10 include two other BRIC[2] languages (Portuguese and Hindi), and the tongues of two economic heavyweights (Germany and Japan).

The Power Language Index is an assessment of the influence of a language on the global stage. The power dynamics within a given region, country, city, etc. will be unique to their own situation. For example, in Aruba—a former Dutch colony situated in Latin America—the most powerful languages are Dutch, Papiamento (local language), Spanish, and English (in large part because of tourism).

This index is a snapshot in time on the power of languages. It does not reflect on past trends or assess trajectories. Nevertheless, it is likely that the score of Mandarin Chinese would have been lower ten years ago. Likewise, its value ten years from now is likely to be higher.

Dealing with the Chinese languages poses certain difficulties. For one, some would argue that the collection of Chinese languages are actually one language and should be viewed as dialects of this one language. Given the mutual intelligibility of (some of) the variants of Chinese most linguists would disagree. Nevertheless, none of the Chinese languages other than Mandarin Chinese and Cantonese have any kind of official status—even in the case of Cantonese, its official status in Hong Kong is peculiar as Hong Kong itself has become a special administrative region (SAR) of China and has never been a member of the UN. Moreover, there is ambiguity (purposely) in Hong Kong in which Chinese (Cantonese versus Mandarin) is considered the official language. And China's policy of promoting Mandarin Chinese (Putonghua), even at the expense of the other variants of Chinese, detracts from much of the efficacy of the other Chinese languages. For historical reasons and because of the large Cantonese diaspora and the prominence of Hong Kong, Cantonese is typically viewed outside of China as the alternative variant of Chinese. Moreover, Cantonese has a rich number of valid indicators to measure its efficacy, whereas the other variants of Chinese do not.

Similarly, Hindi and Urdu are essentially the same language but use different scripts and have since their split (the partition of India and Pakistan) developed their own unique features. Moreover, there are various dialects of Hindi which are often classified as languages. Putting these languages under the umbrella of Hindi would significantly raise its number of native speakers and extend its scope.

Given the above, the PLI results are presented in the Appendix under the following conditions: (1) the Chinese languages are all lumped into one ('Chinese'), with the exception of Cantonese, and (2) the Hindustan languages (Indo-Aryan Central Zone) are all grouped as one ('Hindi'). This change reduces the count of languages in the PLI to 113.

With the Chinese (except Cantonese) and Hindi languages each taken collectively, the rank ordering of languages catapults Hindi from 10th to 8th place. But the higher count of native speakers of Chinese does not change its rank, as there is a big gap between 2nd and 1st ranking. Cantonese, the lone 'other' Chinese language, places 11th just ahead of Italian.

Top-10 Languages

English

English is the world's *lingua franca*. Its dominance as the global means of communication is unrivalled. It is (by the measure of the PLI) more than twice as effective as its nearest rival (Mandarin Chinese). It is the leading language in each of the five opportunities opened by language.

The rise of English as the most important powerful language is spurred by the economic dominance and geographic reach of the English-speaking countries, a legacy of the British Empire that gave rise to many modern-day powerhouse nations. Most notably, the USA are the world's economic, cultural and military superpower, and the UK, along with Canada, are also leading nations (G7) themselves.

The 'neutrality' of English has also helped spur its usage and uptake. For example, in both India and Singapore it was chosen to be an official language and means of cross-group communication without favouring any particular group. Likewise, rival continental European nations, or even different linguistic groups in the same country, often prefer to communicate in English rather than in a rival European language. For example, Swiss of German and French backgrounds often prefer to communicate in English rather than capitulate to conversing in the counterpart's (rival) tongue.

Globalisation is synonymous with English. The consequent anglification of cultures threatens to displace lesser languages and even threatens other powerful languages.

Mandarin

Mandarin Chinese is the second most powerful language, edging out French. Its rise on the global stage is a recent phenomenon. Mandarin was hardly spoken outside of China until recent years; China itself had remained largely outside of the modern global economy until economic reforms were ushered in post-Mao. However, Mandarin remains far behind English, though its prominence is growing. Nevertheless, it is a regional language, with its uptake outside of Greater China limited mostly to the Chinese diaspora and expatriate communities. Its script-based and tonal nature has limited its uptake—most of the world functions in an alphabetic (especially Latin) language and without the use of tones.

There are two modern written forms of Chinese: traditional and simplified. Simplified has been used in China since circa 1950s as part of the Chinese government's scheme to promote greater literacy. Traditional characters are used in Taiwan, Hong Kong and Macau. Singapore—where Mandarin was not native—opted to install Mandarin (with simplified Chinese) as its official Chinese language when it was established (to avoid the language politics of competing Chinese languages there).

French

French is the third most powerful language, buttressed by its strong standing in diplomatic circles. Indeed, French is the go-to second language (English being the global first language) people acquire when they seek to distinguish themselves. The language of De Gaulle holds official status at most major international organisations (and all tracked in the PLI), even if English happens to be the *de facto* working tongue. Nevertheless, where English and French once vied against each other to be the global *lingua franca*, French has clearly slipped behind its cross-Channel rival.

French punches above its weight relative to its small base of native speakers. The language counts just 80 million speakers, the smallest of the top-10 languages. But the power of French can be seen in its high number of L2 speakers (trailing only English and Arabic). Indeed, French is the *lingua franca* or the language of the elite in many African nations even if it is not the mother tongue of the population at large.

Spanish

Spanish places just behind French, but the trajectory going forward may soon have French eclipsed by its Romance-language rival as Latin America is steadily growing. In terms of number of native speakers it trails just Mandarin. On the global diplomatic stage it trails just English and French in facilitating global communication. Nevertheless, its global reach is limited by its geography as it is spoken only in Europe and Latin America.

Amongst the five opportunities Spanish fares worst on 'Knowledge & Media'. But this is more a consequence of the dominance of English in this sphere rather than a shortcoming, per se, of the Spanish language. Nevertheless, the quality of institutions of higher learning—and ergo the research and knowledge they embody—in the Spanish-speaking world lags behind that of those with English, French or German roots.

Arabic

Arabic is the fifth most powerful language. It is spoken primarily in the Middle East and North Africa (MENA), but its status as the language of the Quran compels many Muslims worldwide to study it. For this reason, it counts 250 million L2 speakers, second only to English. The strength of Arabic is also supported by the prosperous economies of oil-rich Arab nations, a phenomenon that may retreat as the price of oil has fallen sharply since peaking in 2014.

Amongst the top-10 languages, Arabic is the laggard in the 'Knowledge & Media' opportunity, primarily on the aspect of knowledge. Modern higher education and research are still nascent in the region, and the political and cultural climate currently is not quite conducive to the modern research university. Colonial legacy has also given rise to French (and in modern times English) as the most prestigious language in some Arabic countries.

Russian

Russian is the primary language of Russia, but is also widely spoken in many of the former Soviet states (and satellite states), where large Russian diaspora communities also exist. In spite of recent economic and political shocks, Russia remains a globally important nation (nuclear power, permanent member of the UN Security Council, etc.) and the vast geography of the nation (and its resource riches) give it a good foundation to grow (notwithstanding political issues).

Russian uses the Cyrillic alphabet, in contrast to the other influential European languages which use the Latin script. Soviet legacy has expanded the use of Cyrillic, where it is the form of writing in Kazakh and Mongolian amongst other places. Nevertheless, there is a push in some of these nations—and even within Russia—to adopt the Latin script.

German

German places seventh on the PLI on the strength of the German-speaking economies. Indeed, the per capita wealth of German-speaking nations ($47,192) is the highest amongst all language groups. But the influence of the German language is limited by its small geographic coverage, being spoken (in large numbers) only in Western Europe. Nevertheless, the prominence of German may rise as the post-Brexit EU will see less influence of UK (and ergo English language) culture on the continent. Likewise, a strong economy has made the country an attractive destination for migrants and refugees.

The relatively limited influence of German is in some ways rather self-imposed, as German speakers seldom 'compel' the language on foreigners (in contrast to French speakers). Indeed, in many professional settings Germans will switch to English to accommodate even the presence of just one non-German speaker in the group.

Hindi

Hindi is the dominant language of India, but India is also home to hundreds of other languages. This has given rise to a situation in which the influence of Hindi has been limited as the Government of India needs to placate the concerns of competing languages. Indeed, Hindi punches well below its weight (in contrast to French) relative to its number of native speakers (310 million).

The language politics of India have limited the ability of the country to promote its most prolific native language. Indeed, competition across the various linguistic factions in India (and the history of English colonialism) has helped spur the rise of English in India (and globally). With no internal push from India to promote the use of Hindi, either within the country or internationally, the language will remain low on the international radar in spite of it being the dominant language of the world's second most populous nation and third largest economy (PPP).

Japanese

Japanese is the most isolated of the top-10 languages. It is spoken in just one country, which is itself an (isolated) island nation. The complexity of the language (for most foreign learners)—it uses three writing systems (katakana, hiragana and kanji) as well as the Latin alphabet for transliterations—has limited the uptake of the language as a second language. Nevertheless, the popularity of Japanese popular culture, especially with respect to anime, has gained it a sizeable number of students studying the language.

Declining birth rates and lack of immigration in the country will cause a sharp drop in the population of Japan over the next century. Combined with the economic stagnation of the economy, these circumstances suggest that the influence of the Japanese language will wane over time. However, as the strength of (Mandarin) Chinese grows there may be scope for Japanese to leverage its strength—kanji are Chinese characters used in Japanese (albeit not necessarily with the same meaning).

Portuguese

Along with English, the Portuguese language is now more prominent outside of its historic homeland (Portugal). The diversity of its geography is second only to English: Portuguese is spoken on four continents. Portuguese is also a close cousin of Spanish (and it is claimed that Portuguese speakers are better able to understand Spanish than vice versa), so Portuguese speakers will also gain in a world where the prominence of Spanish grows.

The trajectory of Portuguese hinges a lot on the fate and success of Brazil, a BRIC nation. The re-emergence of Portuguese in East Timor is one of the few exceptions going against the anglification phenomenon. Indeed, when East Timor gained independence, the choice for Portuguese as official language came as a bit of a surprise as English and/or Indonesian seemed like more logical choices to promote as official languages.

Country PLI-Score

The PLI assesses and compares the efficacy of languages. But every country has a language profile. Nations derive a part of their competitiveness based on their language capabilities. English-speaking countries enjoy the benefit that the world conducts business in their tongue. And as English is the world's *lingua franca* it means that talent can easily flow there. Moreover, English speakers can easily travel and work abroad as English is the second language in virtually every country (where it is not already native). It is no wonder that eight of the top-10 global financial centres are English-speaking/proficient cities.

However, at the same time it is very powerful to speak other languages. A country with capabilities in English and Mandarin—the numbers one and two PLI languages—would be able to engage with a large part of the world. Better yet would be a multilingual society that speaks English, Mandarin and French.

It is possible to calculate the 'language dividend' of nations as the weighted average of the PLI scores based on the profile of languages spoken there. For example, in Switzerland the language profile looks as follows:[3]

Table 1.3: Language Profile Switzerland

LANGUAGE	SHARE (%)	PLI SCORE
German	67.6	0.191
French	23.8	0.338
Italian	8.6	0.108

Thus the country PLI score for Switzerland is the weighted average of the PLIs that prevail: 0.228. For the unilingual United States, the country PLI would be 0.889. But is the gap between the two really that expansive? Most people in Switzerland are able to speak English. This should be reflected in the country's PLI outcome.

The country PLI score needs to take into consideration that English is the global *lingua franca*. This can be done by adjusting the weighted-average PLI score by the nation's level of English proficiency. Fortunately, there is a handy measure for this: the English Proficiency Index (EPI).[4] Using the EPI, the country PLI can be calculated as the weighted average PLI plus the English proficiency score of the share of non-native English speakers.[5]

The country PLI can be interpreted as the efficacy with which the average citizen/resident of that nation can engage the world by virtue of their language ability. For example, although Chinese citizens speak the second most powerful language, their low proficiency in English makes them less effective in engaging outside of Greater China—they rank 41st in the country PLI. Singapore, on the other hand, actually has a country PLI score higher than the English PLI score (0.889) because its residents speak English, Mandarin, Malay and Tamil. For those whose native tongue is not already English, they possess a high proficiency in it.[6]

An alternative measure of the language dividend of a society might be to measure the number of languages effectively spoken in a city/region. That is, for a given place (typically a city or metropolitan area), we might consider a language to be active if there are at least 10,000 speakers. In the case of the UAE, there are 35 active languages and the sum of the PLI scores of the active languages is 3.440 making it one of the most linguistically powerful (and diverse) places in the world.

Individual PLI-Score

A caveat of the country PLI score is that it ignores multilinguals and only considers English as a second language. Calculating the country PLI is a difficult exercise because it requires to fully characterize the degree of multilingualism of all the residents of a country. However, it can be done at an individual level with relative ease. Consider a person with the following language profile where proficiency is assessed using the Common European Framework of Reference for Languages (CEFR) scale:

Table 1.4: Language Profile Scores

LANGUAGE	LEVEL / CEFR	FLUENCY SCORE	PLI SCORE
English	Native or bilingual	1.00	0.889
Cantonese	B2	0.75	0.116
French	B2	0.75	0.337
German	B1	0.50	0.191
Mandarin	B1	0.50	0.411
Russian	A2	0.25	0.244

If we assign a fluency score ranging from 0.25 for A2 with 0.25 increments at each CEFR level, up to 1.00 for C1/C2, then the individual PLI score is the weighted sums of the language profile PLIs (1.591 in the example above). The score can be interpreted as a measure of how easily a multilingual person could engage the world by virtue of their language facilities. It is also a way to compare the efficacy of multilinguals with different language profiles. A polyglot who speaks (only) French, Italian, Portuguese and Spanish (all fluently) is much less powerful (from a global perspective) in languages than a polyglot who speaks (only) English, Mandarin, Russian and Arabic (all fluently)—with scores of 0.893 vs 1.817, respectively. In fact, an English-Mandarin bilingual (PLI score of 1.300) is more effective than a Romance languages polyglot.

Notes

1. As in Table 1.1, the '*'-symbol signifies that half weight is attributed to this indicator within the opportunity.

2. BRIC is an acronym for the countries of Brazil, Russia, India, and China that was popularized in 2001 by Jim O'Neil, an economist with the investment bank Goldman Sachs at the time
3. Certain simplifying assumptions are made, including overlooking multilingualism.
4. Education First English Proficiency Index (2016).
5. To scale the EPI to be comparable with the PLI, the EPI score is averaged with the share of native English speakers in a given country.
6. Mandarin is the official Chinese language used in Singapore, although many of its residents actually speak as native one of the other variants of the Chinese languages/dialects.

Manuel Célio Conceição

Higher Education Language Policies: Global Trends and Local Needs

Higher education language policies (HELP) are supposed to be part of the institutional strategy for the internationalisation of universities. They should define the language regime for teaching, research, knowledge transfer to society and for governance aspects. In reality, languages are mostly absent from policy documents and internationalisation often means anglification. In this chapter, we will discuss the concept of HELP, within the framework of the current globalized context higher education institutions (HEI) function in. Higher education (HE) activity must have impact not only at international level but also (perhaps above all) at local/regional/national level. Languages and HELP are conditions for maintaining and promoting this dichotomy. Language has to be considered as "languaging" with different variants and varieties (established or emergent). It is a process rather than a product. Language diversity is not a barrier and must be seen as a real asset, avoiding national (regional, minority) languages from being lost and promoting multidimensionality of knowledge creation, access, and dissemination.

Keywords: higher education, language policy, multilingualism, globalisation, internationalisation, universities

Higher education (HE), as other structures of our societies, is nowadays under pressure caused by a growth of the local and global dichotomy. Globalisation, mobility, inclusion and respect for identities and local specificities are changing the social organisation and demanding answers to emergent questions. On the one hand, higher education institutions (HEI) must be competitive and have a role at the international level. Internationalisation is an essential item in all their strategies. On the other hand, a real impact of HEI activity is asked at the local level. In both cases, HE is supposed to contribute to the improvement of life conditions, and to solve individual and social problems. The main areas in HE activity—teaching, research, and the transfer of knowledge to society—as well as governance will never be developed without a proper language policy. This chapter intends to discuss the question of higher education language policy (HELP) under the present conceptions of internationalisation, the new epistemological approaches of language and language sciences and the relationship between language and science.

Internationalisation

As Helms and Brajkovic (2017) explain, internationalisation can cover a range of activities going from traditional collaborations to partnerships to articulated institutional commitment. It includes student and staff mobility, faculty and research centres policies and practices, shared curriculum and learning outcomes and administrative leadership, structure and staffing. In this century, more and more European universities started with joint projects and programmes and are now, for example, working under the European Universities Initiative.[1] The role of HE in society cannot only be to reproduce knowledge, but it must also include creating knowledge, finding solutions to problems that, in some cases, do not exist yet. Collaboration and mobility can play an important part in this, as they reshape HE creating complex contexts. There are new trends that have become increasingly more present in the last few years. Davey et al. (2018, p. 7) refer to the trends identified by McKinsey:

> The consultancy firm McKinsey identified four global megatrends, 'global shifts reshaping the world', which will impact society over the years to come:
>
> - Emerging markets and Urbanisation
> - Trade, people, finance, and data: Greater global connections
> - Accelerating technological change
> - Responding to the challenges of an aging world

These trends are changing the HE landscape and imposing a new analysis of the concept of university education and its relevance and impact.

Universities and other institutions of HE have suffered from some instrumentalisation, requiring them to be submitted to economic, cultural and even commercial hegemonies in which the primary criterion seems to be of a financial and budgetary nature, associated with the question of indispensable utilitarianism. The pretext of internationalisation and the competitiveness that comes from it, which overlaps with the somewhat naïve (when taken at face value) collaborative intention, leads to a standardisation of strategies, practices, rhetoric and linguistic uses that can be analysed in the framework of an apparent Americanisation and recolonisation, a 'westernisation'. Sperduti (2017) wrote that the function of the university is not only to produce new knowledge but also to preserve what was historically accumulated. The fact is that the standardisation makes epistemic procedures and models disappear, which is why "researchers [...] must be aware of the systematics and continued privilege of certain knowledge, and particularly in global settings that have historically been colonized and continue to be Othered in the present" (Sperduti 2017, p. 11).

Internationalisation is not a new aspect of higher education, as universities have always been international. However, internationalisation does need new approaches, since it has become a vital need for institutions. Mobility of students and staff, university campuses abroad, Erasmus programmes, advertisements to attract international students, higher education fairs, international research teams and networks, rankings: these are all reasons for considering internationalisation as one of the most important lines in all institutional strategic plans. The standardisation of internationalisation can lead to a decrease in mobility if academic curricula and practices begin to resemble. However, some standardisation is necessary for mobility strategies in order to allow accreditation and validation of competencies and of expected results agreed by different actors. One limitation for mobility can be the growth of movements that, under the designation of internationalisation, promote transnational education and training with resources for digital and non-presential learning; a type of virtual mobility. Geographic distances between people (and communities and cultures) are erased by virtualisation in the global world. Almost all of us can participate in individual mobility projects without having to get out of the context in which we have always lived. Still, the benefits and drawbacks of mobility have an impact on everyone, even in our 'own' context.

Universities were created with the clear intention to be universal, as is expressed even by the etymology of the designation, but their relevance has always been understood, first and foremost, under the local/international dichotomy. The massification of access to HE, and the subsequent creation of competitive mechanisms that ignore political, geographical, thematic, and linguistic borders, have altered the initial perspectives of the concept of internationalisation, as it now even assumes a tendency to have an economic and financial character. Internationalisation has been, for at least two decades (particularly in the last one), a very common term in all strategic university plans.

Internationalisation involves several processes, forms of implementation and impacts. It has to be present in all aspects of HE, going from teaching and research to issues of knowledge transfer and the relationship with society and governance itself. Evidence of internationalisation can be seen by commitments and agreements of inter-institutional relations, action plans of the leadership at all levels, curricular structuring and definition of learning outcomes across cycles, the definition of research plans, the mobility of students and staff, collaborations, partnerships and networks, etc. A wide and broad conception of internationalisation allows for different approaches, inspired in Knight (1996), namely:

- internationalisation as a process and activity that is verified by the decisions made concerning governance, curricular changes or strategies related to the mobility, for example;
- internationalisation for the development of competences, especially in relation to interculturality;
- internationalisation as ethos that consubstantiates evidences of cultures and permissive practices of international activities.

The internationalisation of HE causes transformations on an individual, institutional and even national level, leading to a recontextualisation of disciplinary and academic cultures into the evolutionary framework of a global culture, as defined by Djerasimovic (2016).

HELP

While having mentioned the concept of internationalisation and its scope in the landscape of HE and the fact that it is an important element of HEI strategies, there is little evidence that these strategies explicitly deal with an important condition for and one of the main issues with internationalisation, namely the language issue. When present, strategies have a special focus on economic and financial impact (attracting international students, whose tuition fees are significantly higher). The implementation of any strategy of internationalisation has an organisational impact, as mentioned above. Internationalisation is not only a desire or a goal sought by institutions, students and staff, but it must also be considered as constituting the essence of HE. In internationalisation strategies—which often include quantified goals, as in partnerships to be implemented, number of people whose mobility is intended to be encouraged, etc.—the question of language or languages is unequivocally central. The definition of language policies and their relationship with the organisation at all levels (teaching, research, extension, governance, etc.) are key elements of internationalisation.

The changes which occurred in different aspects of HEI and the massive entrance of students from different geographies and from non-traditional groups (Conceição 2018) represent a challenge for university autonomy. They impose the need to overcome tradition and conservatism, since they are a determinant factor of de-traditionalisation, framed in what Giddens (1994) called reflexive modernisation. Considering these new paradoxes (local vs. global, autochthonous students vs. mobility or international students, etc.) and given that they can be sources of conflict, the need for political measures to avoid or to solve them is undeniable. A language policy is one of these important measures, while it is not even referred in the majority of institutional documents, as shown, for example, by Pinto and Araújo e Sá (2019).

Under these conditions of a changing society and all the changes occurring in HE (new publics, internationalisation, competitiveness, mobility, etc.), decisions about languages are crucial for institutional development, for quality criteria and for attracting new students and staff. A real and effective HELP is needed. HELP is the set of decisions and measures (more or less explicit), in a given institution, about the use of languages in all aspects of its activity. Languages in HE have often been the elephant in the room. Not only must the concept of language be properly perceived, but there is also the myth that everyone in HE can use English. Even language centres have strategic plans to answer to these recent needs. However, their activity as language courses providers is repeatedly seen as secondary. HELP can be put in place to deal with these issues effectively.

Language under the current epistemological framework (more or less inspired by Saussurean and Chomskyan ideas) has been conceived as a set of *paroles*/ performances shared by a community, a social group. This concept is based on individualism, in selfhood. It is a persona-centric model that characterizes the Western philosophy after Descartes' *cogito ergo sum* ('I think, therefore I am'). In the last few years, perspectives on languages have been inspired in emergent uses, practices and needs, in ecolinguistic approaches, and under different metaphysical questions. These perspectives allow for a new epistemological approach that reinforces the community topic. In the Ubuntu philosophy, for example, as a communo-centric approach, "a human being achieves humanity through his or her relations with other human beings" (Eze 2011, p. 12).[2] Thus, the concept of language must be seen as a practice under a post-normative approach, and as languaging (Love 2017) and translanguaging to create equity relations with others.[3]

This new conception of language, not about systematicity, regularities and grammatical conceptualisations, is much more comprehensive and multidimensional. Language is not only a tool for communication, but also a *locus* for knowledge. In language, with language, from language, we acquire, we build, we create, we transmit, and we disseminate knowledge. Under this complex conception, when talking about my language(s) and others' language(s), the otherness should be reformulated; what speakers and languages have in common must be emphasized, not their differences. This is also a question of respect and of democracy, as Maalouf (1998, p. 53) said "Si celui dont j'étudie la langue ne respecte pas la mienne, parler sa langue cesse d'être un geste d'ouverture, il devient un acte d'allégeance et de soumission." ("If the language of what I'm studying doesn't respect my own, speaking the language stops being a sign of openness and rather becomes an act of allegiance and submission.")

In HE, languages can have different statuses, for instance as language of instruction, language of research, language for internal/external communication, languages taught in content and language integrated learning (CLIL), languages taught as subject, etc. Therefore, the approach must be differentiated and the linguistic goal, with respect for linguistic and multilingual repertoires, must be the improvement of multilingual competence (Conceição et al., 2018a; Caruso 2019).

As HE is more and more open to all sorts of contexts (physical and geographical or virtual, local or global, personal or institutional, etc.) and as languages (at least, some of them) have been commodified, the apparently easiest way to solve the communicative problems, is to reduce language diversity to the so-called *lingua franca*:

> Les argumentaires en faveur de l'anglicisation sont bien rodés [...] mais le fait est qu'elle s'impose le plus souvent sans qu'il soit besoin d'argumenter longuement: elle se fait spontanément, dans l'inconscience collective, ce qui est sans doute le signe qu'il se passe quelque chose de subliminal au niveau anthropologique. ('The arguments in favour of English are well-honed, but most oftenly it imposes itself without having to argue long: it does so spontaneously, in the collective subconscious, which no doubt means something subliminal on an anthropological level is taking place.') (Frath 2017, p. 114)

This, however, leads to language loss, domain loss, inequities and disrespect towards students and staff as well as disciplinary and historical cultural and rhetorical specificities.

In HE, the sold panacea seems to be 'all in English'. Real-world observation and research results show that a reduction to monolingualism (English) is a very problematic choice. Jensen et al. (2009) and de Wit (2017) gave us examples:

> An increased use of English in higher education may result in difficulties for the general public in keeping abreast of scientific advancements. The second opposing theme is related to domain loss. As more and more people are educated through the medium of English, they may find it more difficult to discuss their field in Danish. In the long term, the increasing use of English may mean that Danish can no longer be used to disseminate or discuss academic subjects because the discipline specific terminology will be neglected and will not develop. The third opposing theme focuses on the concern that an increased use of English in the classroom will negatively affect the quality of instruction because neither the Danish lecturers nor the Danish students are working to their full potential since English is a foreign language for both parties. Instruction may be less precise or teaching methodology may be compromised. (Jensen et al., 2009, p. v)

English-language instruction appears to have a negative impact on students with a migration background and on students from a disadvantaged background (de Wit 2017).

Multilingual Competence

From a didactic point of view, arguments for monolingualism (all in English) are that in such a case, mobility between institutions and countries is easier for all, and standardisation is supposed to facilitate the transmission of knowledge. Arguments in favour of a multilingual approach are (again from a didactic point of view) the increased ease to connect with scientific and cultural traditions, the enhancement of creativity, and the connection of university research and scientists with local needs.

Reactions to the anglification process are becoming stronger, but the fact is that other languages have been given less interest, usage, space and power in HE. It is known that the use of English decreases the quality of teaching and learning and creates inequality in conditions to access to funds for research. Additionally, it makes it more difficult for research results, published in English in scientific journals, to have an impact at the local and national level.

Across Europe, formal activities of teaching and research in HE are becoming monolingual, because they gravitate towards the use of a single *lingua franca* (Conceição et al., 2018b). Under the guise of internationalisation, English as a *lingua franca* (or as a *lingua academica*) is used as a solution to attract students from abroad or to prepare students to act as global players and in different contexts—as if English were used in all those different contexts. However, campuses are increasingly multilingual, and learning spaces are multilingual and multicultural, frequently combining a local or a national language with a *lingua franca* and other languages.

Students, professors, researchers and other staff travel around with different types of mobility-enhancing programmes. There is a huge and largely hidden capital of linguistic and cultural diversity that is not used and even forgotten by institutions. In order to ensure unrestricted access to knowledge and to different scientific and academic cultures, appropriate attention to these resources is required. The linguistic repertoires of different actors should be taken into consideration through the use of multilingual lectures, intercomprehensive approaches and/or translanguaging strategies. Through the use of different languages, access to concepts and knowledge and terminology harmonisation are easier, since linguistic competence is a condition for content-knowledge competence.

When language diversity is still a fact in HE, languages are usually used in separate situations, in what might be called a segregated way. Having a structured HELP allows HEI to develop the maintenance of diversity and it would encourage students, researchers and administrative staff to better manage, develop, and use the various languages in their repertoire.

> The repertoire in its entirety represents a resource enabling action in diverse use situations. It evolves across time and experience throughout life and includes growth in intercultural awareness and ability to cope with, and participate in, multicultural contexts of academic study and working life. (MAGICC Conceptual Framework 2013, p. 5[4])

Knowledge is acquired, built and transferred through languages. University classrooms are frequently and artificially monolingual. Some local/national and heritage languages are typically seen as not scientifically relevant, and the impact of HE activity on the local context frequently appears to be underestimated or ignored. These are examples of what Skutnabb-Kangas (1988, p. 13) calls linguicism, a set of "ideologies, structures and practices which are used to legitimate, effectuate, regulate and reproduce an unequal division of power and resources (both material and immaterial) between groups which are defined on the basis of language."

The Global and the Local

Multilingual competence, seen under new and emergent voices of multilingualism, has a double dimension: cognitive and social. It has been approached under the ambiguity between the global (multilingual but presented as monolingual in English) and the local (monolingual by tradition and law—in some cases where state language, first language or language of instruction/schooling is imposed, but, in reality, multilingual). The multilingual ethos is, thus, more and more an almost universal specificity of the HE education population (students and staff) and the HE landscape (campuses, websites, etc.). HELP must enhance the dichotomy between the "regional location" and the "international orientation" (Conceição et al., 2018c). In order to achieve this double need—summarized as the tension between the local and the global—strategies to promote the local culture(s) and language(s) and to foster the international dimension of HEI must be designed and implemented to promote an intercultural and multilingual education, in order to avoid what Eze (2017) called "cosmopolitanism in the age of xenophobia".

HE must be multilingual because language diversity is an asset and education should not be reduced to monolingual practices. Multilingual competences ought to be promoted by HELP, which is designed in context-driven approaches and includes strategies to maintain language diversity. A balance between a *lingua franca* (including English-medium instruction) and instruction in local/ national languages is needed, while also making space for students' and staffs' own linguistic repertoires.

The contradiction between the imposition of one dominant language and the existence and development of multilingual and multicultural educational and social spaces, or in other words, the tension between global trends and local needs, epitomizes the relevance of the variety and multidimensionality of visions and approaches generated by linguistic diversity. None of the expected roles of higher education, neither at local nor at global levels, will be maintained without the continuing support or the development of the local/national language!

Notes

1. See online: https://ec.europa.eu/education/education-in-the-eu/european-education-area/european-universities-initiative_en.
2. Ubuntu is a Bantou word which means 'I am because we are'.
3. Brock-Utne (2016) presents translanguaging under the ubuntu paradigm.
4. See online: www.magicc.eu.

References

Brock-Utne, Birgit, 'The Ubuntu Paradigm on Curriculum Work, Language of Instruction and Assessment', *International Review of Education*, 62/1 (2016), 29–44.

Caruso, Elisa, 'A Competência Multilingue no Ensino Superior', doctoral dissertation, Universidade do Algarve, Faro, 2019.

Conceição, Manuel Célio, 'Prefácio', in António Fragoso, coord., *Estudantes Não-tradicionais no Ensino Superior* (Coimbra: CINEP/IPC, 2018), 11–18.

Conceição, Manuel Célio, et al., 'How Can Be Fostered Through Multilingualism in Higher Education (HE)?', in François Grin et al., ed., *The MIME Vademecum* <www.mime-project.org> (2018a), 120–121.

Conceição, Manuel Célio, et al., 'What Is the Role of English in Multilingual and Multicultural Learning Spaces', in François Grin et al., ed., *The MIME Vademecum* <www.mime-project.org> (2018b), 140–141.

Conceição, Manuel Célio, et al., 'Why Is It Advisable to Combine "International Orientation" with "Regional Location" in the Language Strategy of Universities?', in François Grin et al., ed., *The MIME Vademecum* <www.mime-project.org> (2018c), 130–131.

Davey, Todd, et al., eds, *The Future of Universities thoughtbook* (Amsterdam: University Industry Innovation Network, 2018).

Djerasimovic, Sanja, 'Examining the Discourses of Cross-cultural Communication in Transnational Higher Education: From Imposition to Transformation', in Catherine Montgomery, ed., *Transnational and Transcultural Positionality in Globalised Higher Education*, (London: Routledge, 2016), 8–20.

Eze, Michael Onyebuchi, 'I Am Because You Are', *The UNESCO Courier* 64/4 (2011), 10–13.

Eze, Michael Onyebuchi., 'I Am Because You Are: Cosmopolitanism in the Age of Xenophobia', *Philosophical Papers* 46/1 (2017), 85–109.

de Wit, Hans, 'The Complex Politics of Teaching in English in HE', University World News (2017), <http://www.universityworldnews.com/article.php?story=20170829100757301>.

Frath, Pierre, 'L'Anglicisation comme Phénomène Anthropologique', in Françoise Le Lièvre et al., eds, *Langues et Cultures dans L'Internationalisation de L'Enseignement Supérieur—Languages and Cultures in the Internationalization of Higher* Education (Frankfurt am Main: Peter Lang, 2017), 114–129.

Jensen, Christian, et al., 'Underviseres Holdninger til Engelsk som Undervisningssprog – En Spørgeskemaundersøgelse på Københavns Universitet', Center for Internationalisering og Parallelsproglighed Københavns Universitet (2009), <https://cip.ku.dk/pdf/publ/Underviseres_holdninger_til_engelsk_som_undervisningssprog.pdf/>.

Giddens, Anthony, 'Living in a Post-traditional Society', in Ulrich Beck et al., orgs, *Reflexive Modernization, Politics, Tradition and Aesthetics in the Modern Social Order* (Stanford: Stanford University Press, 1994), 56–109.

Knight, Jane, 'Internationalisation of Higher Education', paper presented at the Internationalisation of Higher Education in the Asia-Pacific Region Conference, Melbourne (1996), 7–9.

Love, Nigel, 'On Languaging and Languages', *Language Sciences* 61 (2017), 113–147.

Maalouf, Amin, *Les Identités Meurtrières* (Paris : Editions Grasset & Fasquelle, 1998).

Pinto, Susana, and Maria Helena Araújo e Sá, 'Language Education Policy in Portuguese Public Universities: The Voices of Institutional Stakeholders', *Current Issues in Language Planning* 20/2 (2019), 140–159.

Skutnabb-Kangas, Tove, 'Multilingualism and the Education of Minority Children', in Tove Skutnabb-Kangas and Jim Cummins, eds, *Minority Education: From Shame to Struggle* (Avon: Multilingual Matters, 1988), 9–44.

Sperduti, Vanessa, 'Internationalization as Westernization in Higher Education', *Comparative & International Education* 9 (2019), 9–12.

Part II European Case Studies: Central Europe, the Baltic Area, and the Nordic Countries

Ivan Svetlik and Monika Kalin Golob

Small Is Sensitive: The Case of Internationalisation and Language Utilisation in Slovenian Higher Education

The chapter starts with an introduction in which the tension between national and foreign language use will be defined as a problem of contemporary public universities, as they are on the one hand expected to protect and develop national cultures and languages, and on the other to verify and share their research results in the international scientific and student communities. The major part of the chapter is devoted to national language and internationalisation policies as they have been formulated in policy documents and legislation. The Slovenian language policy document has been in place for some decades and requires several measures of national language protection and development. The policy document on the internationalisation of higher education has been accepted only recently with the aim to enhance international activities of higher education institutions. It seems, however, that both documents are not well coordinated. The chapter concludes with the example of language and internationalisation policy implementation as they have been practised at the University of Ljubljana. It becomes clear that the university must often find its own way out of contradictory policy requirements if it wants to fulfil its scientific and national identity missions.

Keywords: higher education, internationalisation, language policy, national language, universities, identity, Slovenia, Central Europe

Historical Perspective

The first European universities were established in the Middle Ages in line with a cosmopolitan and universalistic model (Perkin 2007; Gacel-Avila 2005). Scholars and students were coming from different parts of Europe and other continents, and were moving between universities as “wandering scholars” (Kerr 1990). This was made possible due to the utilisation of Latin as a common language of all scholars and students irrespective of their ethnic origin. An important contextual condition was that practically all universities of that time were embedded in the Christian cultural and institutional settings promoted and defended by the Catholic Church.

A radical change occurred in the seventeenth century as a consequence of the expansion of Protestantism and the formation of nation states. Universities were transformed from cosmopolitan into national institutions. They had to serve national interests and thus became important centres of the national culture and the national language (Nokkala 2007). Scholars and students were increasingly recruited nationally. Studies abroad were not allowed in many states. Academic staff became a constitutive part of national elites. Latin was gradually substituted for national languages.

The model of national universities with the accent on the development and utilisation of the national language dominated for some centuries in parallel to the proliferation of the nation states. In Europe British, French and German university models became most known and were exported to the rest of the world (de Wit 2002), including the use of the national language in teaching, especially in the period of colonialism.

In the twentieth century, particularly in the second half, the model of inwardly oriented national universities started to show increasing deficiencies. It could not support new developments towards the reconciliation of international conflicts after the Second World War and decolonisation, nor the globalisation of the economy or the establishment of the new world order through international economic and political organisations. Universities started to internationalize their activities due to socio-cultural, political, economic and academic reasons (Knight 2007).

The internationalisation of universities has been perceived to strengthen their position in the international academic community and academic markets, thus strengthening the position of national states in the global world; not as a substitution of universities' national functions. Universities have retained their responsibility for addressing national specific research issues, for educating young generations and preparing them for the national labour market, and for nurturing the national culture and language(s). However, the international shift has brought to the surface some tensions between services to the nation and the international orientation of universities. Should universities respond in the same way to international and national corporations? Should they equally promote national and other cultures following the concept of multiculturalism? How can they verify their research results if not in the international research community?

Perhaps the most burning issue has arisen with respect to the use of national and other languages. Increasing numbers of foreign and exchange students and of international staff, requirements to prepare graduates to work in internationalized environments either at home or abroad, and a necessity to obtain and verify research results in the international academic community, have opened communication questions. While national interests require universities to nurture the national culture and national language, their internationalisation pushes them towards the use of a new *lingua franca*, i.e. English, for practical and financial reasons.

As Ferguson (2015, p. 4–5) claims, the expansion of English

> has been fuelled by the internationalisation of higher education, a process largely driven by economic forces and, in particular, the emergence of a globalized, competitive market in higher education, as evidenced by the multiplication of University 'league tables' and the competition to attract greater numbers of international students for the fees and increased prestige they bring.

The process of anglification has reached the point where internationalisation of higher education does not promote linguistic pluralism but rather linguistic uniformity; it does not promote multiculturalism but cultural isolation (Fabricius, Mortensen and Haberland 2016). Internationalisation in this form is subverting EU policy of multilingualism and language diversity declared by the Bologna process.

The Issues of Universities' Language Policies in Small and New Nations

The tension between service to the nation and internationalisation seems to be particularly strong at the universities of small and new nations. Several reasons contribute to this.

Small nations have been mostly constituted on an ethnic basis, having their own specific culture and language. Since only a few million and in some cases less than one million people speak their language, it is difficult to expect other nations to understand them without using languages of bigger nations or using a *lingua franca*, such as English. Small nations can be less self-sufficient in all respects, including culture, unless they risk isolation. Therefore they must learn and use foreign languages more than big nations.

Economies of small nations are highly internationalized. Their larger companies produce enough goods for the home markets in a couple of days. Slovenia, for instance, realizes more than two thirds of its gross domestic product on foreign markets. People involved in foreign trade and international industrial cooperation use foreign languages if they want to be successful in acquiring business. Universities preparing graduates for such a professional field are required to convey knowledge of other cultures and languages.

When universities of small nations conduct research it is practically impossible to achieve a critical mass of expertise inside their countries in the majority of science fields. They must cooperate internationally and they must agree on a language that all research partners understand. Research results must be verified by publishing them internationally where "the near hegemony of English research publications" (Ferguson 2015) prevails. The same issue arises in case of international education activities: students sent to other universities must know the language of their hosts, and foreign students, especially exchange students, coming to small nations' universities cannot be expected to know the language of their hosts or to learn it sufficiently unless they study a full programme. This pushes small nations' universities towards using non-national languages to a greater extent than those of bigger nations.

The requirements to internationalize in the fields of economy, education, and science do not always seem to be congruent with one of the main missions of small nations' universities, i.e. to nurture the national culture and language. This mission is of particular importance because small nations in most cases base their national identity on their cultural, artistic, and language traditions and not on their imperial history or military and economic power. Small nations have been rather victims than active proponents of imperial history and globalisation. What creates a particular distinction between them and powerful nations, then, is their culture and language.

For the prosperity of small nations in the future it is of the utmost importance to develop and preserve their languages in their full integrity, meaning that citizens must be able to think and express themselves in their nations' language in all situations and fields of life and work. It is important that people are able to conceive and express their considerations about new situations, new technologies, new organisational solutions, etc. with the words of their own language. The responsibility for the development of these abilities rests on the educational system, particularly universities. Every science and art discipline should conceive and name novelties and convey them to students in their mother tongue.

The tension between caring for the national identity and the need to internationalize is particularly sensitive in the nations which have been fully institutionalized only recently. The Slovenian ethnic community, for instance, already had gotten a translation of the Bible in Slovenian in 1584 (Dalmatin 1584). Since then an increasing number of theatre works, poems and novels were written in Slovenian. The first university—the University of Ljubljana—where Slovenian was used in higher education was established only in 1919. And an independent Slovenian state was created only 72 years after the university, in 1991. One can argue that it was not the state which established the University of Ljubljana but rather the university which contributed the most to the formation of the state of Slovenia by nurturing Slovenian culture and language and by educating Slovene intellectuals in their native language, thus strengthening the feeling of national identity.

It is an unfortunate circumstance that Slovenes have gotten their state and Slovenia has been established as a full and sovereign nation only in the period of globalisation in which nation states delegate some of their sovereignty to international bodies. However, making concessions to the international sphere at the expense of national culture and language nurturing, which seems to be a nation's sacred area and therefore the last area of internationalisation, could be understood as a betrayal of one of the university's core missions. Unlike in some bigger nations, such as the United Kingdom, France, and Germany, where national languages were substituted for Latin, Slovenia and many other small nations were seeking cultural and linguistic independence from bigger nations' cultures and languages. Until Slovenes got their national university in 1919, they were studying mainly in German and Italian. In this respect English is often not perceived as a *lingua franca*, such as Latin before, but as a language of another nation; a language of imperial domination (Phillipson 2015).

The tension between culture and language nurturing and the internationalisation of higher education seeks for reconciliation. A Slovenian approach will be presented in the following paragraphs by describing its language and internationalisation policies.

Language and Internationalisation Policies in Slovenia[1]

The language regulation of higher education in Slovenia was already in place in the period when Slovenia was part of former Yugoslavia. Since independence, the language regulation has derived from various provisions (Accetto 2010, p. 25):

- Article 11 of the Constitution of the Republic of Slovenia defines Slovene as the official language, while in the areas with an Italian and Hungarian national minority official languages are also Italian and Hungarian.
- The Act on Public Usage of Slovene Language (Official Gazette 2004) in article 12 defines that education from preschool to university level is imparted in Slovene, while the use of other languages is permitted in accordance with sector-specific regulations in the field of education. The same Act, in article 13, promotes the learning of Slovene in Slovenia. For that purpose the Government of the Republic of Slovenia has to adopt a programme that will be "in addition to the regular education programmes aimed at language improvement of youth and adult citizens, and programmes aimed at foreign

nationals in Slovenia", as well as special programmes for the promotion of Slovene at foreign education institutions.
- The sector-specific Higher Education Act (MIZŠ 2019) dedicates article 8 to the language of instruction, which is Slovene. However, higher education institutions may provide study programmes or parts of them in a foreign language under the conditions set by their statutes (meaning that foreign language study programmes, parts of study programmes where visiting professors from abroad take part or a significant number of foreign students are enrolled, and study programmes that duplicate the programmes offered in Slovene, can be taught in a foreign language). The Act also defines that higher education institutions "ensure the development of Slovene as a professional or scientific language", that "foreign citizens and Slovenes without Slovene citizenship should be enabled to learn Slovene", and that "the minister responsible for higher education defines the detailed method of how to ensure the development and the learning of Slovene".

Any kind of internationalisation policy of universities is of a much later date. The only available official document on the state level is a 'Strategy of Internationalisation of Slovenian higher education 2016–2020' (MIZŠ 2016). It is understandable that it fosters various kinds of international activities, such as mobility of students and staff, and cooperation in the fields of research and inter-cultural competences development. However, with respect to languages it does not go beyond the above-mentioned legal documents providing general language policy frameworks since it only repeats that along with the openness for communication in foreign languages it is important that universities care for the preservation and development of Slovenian language. The question how to simultaneously achieve internationalisation and national language development remains open. The only added value seems to be a provision of information and education activities for foreign students and staff focused on Slovenian language and culture.

That attention for Slovene does not hinder the quality of internationalisation is shown by the solutions of the 'Resolution on the National Programme for Language Policy 2014–2018' (MK 2015). They build on the assumption that

> Slovene universities and the Republic of Slovenia wish to maintain and further develop Slovene as the language of higher education and the language of science, however, they also wish to provide international dimension of their operation as well as international competitiveness. (p. 28)

The resolution thus defines:

- that the Ministry of Education, Science and Sport and universities, on the basis of the Higher Education Act, the Resolution on the national programme of higher education, and the strategies, should establish transparent modules for a sensible integration of foreign students and higher education teachers: (1) with quality parallel programmes and elective modules, specially formulated for exchange students, with courses that could be selected also by home students providing they meet the required conditions, (2) by introducing the concept of differentiated multilingualism that follows the positive examples from abroad. According to this concept, the language of higher education is equal to the prevailing language of the environment, while simultaneous (machine generated) translation to another language, with instruments and means adapted to individual discipline, should be offered to students who do not master the language of higher education sufficiently. Transparencies and other study materials are generally bilingual, in the language of the environment and in a foreign language, while consultations with foreign students are also held in a foreign language, and (3) by promoting student solidarity and tutorship or partnership between home and foreign students;

- that legislation should define the compulsory majority proportion of higher education programmes offered in the Slovene language, instead of leaving it entirely up to the universities to define. Whereas the strategic orientation of universities and the state regarding the increase of mobility and exchange programmes coincide, the Ministry of Education, Science and Sport and higher education institutions should agree on the adequate method of financing;
- that at the level of doctoral studies universities are given full autonomy regarding their language policy, while taking into account the constitutional and legal restraints and the general principle that Slovene teachers should not lecture Slovene students in a foreign language. (MK 2015, p. 29–30)

This language resolution offers the possibility of including foreign students and teachers, as well as improving the quality of higher education with Slovene and parallel, or specifically developed foreign language subjects and courses. Above all, it preserves the role of Slovene as the language of higher education and science, which should be ensured by responsible national policies.

The draft of a new 'Resolution on the National Programme for Language Policy 2019–2023' confirms the main points of the existing one. A stronger accent is put on the publication of scientific results in Slovenian (and not just foreign) language as a condition for academic promotion at universities.

The 'Resolution on the National Programme for Language Policy 2014–2018' is based on a cosmopolitan view which has been identified in a special research on attitudes towards language utilisation and internationalisation carried out among lecturers and students of the University of Ljubljana. In this research three relatively homogenous groups appeared: the largest pro-Slovene, the smallest pro-English and the medium-sized cosmopolitan. The researchers concluded that the viewpoints of the cosmopolitan group

> are the closest to those that serve as the basis for European and Slovene language policies and for the National Programme 2014–2018. This group of students and lecturers does not strive for the primacy of one of the two languages, but rather for a high proficiency in both languages and for a sensible combination of both. (Kalin Golob et al., 2017)

The research mentioned above reveals highly polarized opinions reflected in an overprotective attitude towards Slovene or in the total lack of consideration regarding the practical and symbolic aspects of language regulation. This seems to be the main reason that there is neither further progress in the elaboration of national language and internationalisation policies nor in their implementation. A situation is created that leads to bypasses, which make the inclusion of foreign students and other dimensions of higher education internationalisation possible. Universities improvise and implement pragmatic and mainly partial solutions.

Language and Internationalisation Policies at the University of Ljubljana

The University of Ljubljana (UL) was founded in 1919 as the first Slovenian university to introduce teaching in the Slovenian language. This was made possible by the collapse of the Austro-Hungarian Empire which had previously opposed such a project, and despite the opinion of the Yugoslav authorities in Belgrade that Ljubljana did not need a university.

The University of Ljubljana was the only Slovenian university for more than five decades; it represented the centre of research and higher education in the country. Its main missions were to nurture basic research, educate young generations and contribute to strengthening the national identity. Initially composed of just five departments (named faculties), it has grown to become a comprehensive university covering all fields of study, today consisting of 23 faculties and three art academies. It retains its leading position in the country with the best international rankings, encompassing around half the research and half the higher education area. It has 39,000 students, about 11.5 % of whom come from outside Slovenia, and nearly 6,000 employees (UL Home Page 2019).

The strengthening of the national identity with the accent on the development of Slovenian terminology has remained one of the core tasks of the UL as it has been outlined in the university's mission statement included in the 'Strategy of the University of Ljubljana 2012–2020' (UL Home Page 2019). Simultaneously

UL has obliged itself to keep pace with the 3 % of the best universities in the world in all fields of its research and education. This obligation requires an increasing internationalisation of university activities. As a consequence UL has accepted its 'Strategy of Internationalisation 2014–2017' (UL Home Page 2019).

At the time of acceptance of the Strategy of Internationalisation, the level of actual internationalisation of UL was rather low. Therefore, it is understandable that the strategy aimed at increasing numbers of:

- foreign students enrolled at the UL;
- exchanged students—incoming and outgoing;
- foreign teachers and researchers;
- exchanged staff—incoming and outgoing;
- programmes and courses taught in English;
- programmes carried out in cooperation with foreign partners or abroad;
- international research projects, particularly EU-financed ones;
- publications in international journals and books;
- citations of works published by UL scholars;
- foreign staff.

The discussion on the goals of the Strategy of Internationalisation pointed out that the activities needed for their fulfilment would mean a significant shift towards wider utilisation of foreign languages in research and teaching/study, particularly English. Several worries were expressed about the protection of Slovenian and about a possible breach of legislation which sets certain limitations to the utilisation of foreign languages. Therefore the strategy included two more points:

- Elaboration of the university's language strategy
- Strengthening of teaching of Slovenian language for foreign students and staff

In the years after the acceptance of the internationalisation strategy, remarkable progress was made in internationalisation at UL. The key indicators presented in Table 3.1 show increasing internationalisation in practically all important fields. In some fields, such as the number of study programmes offered in English, the number of visiting teachers and researchers, the number of foreign students, and the number of citations, achievements significantly surpassed the goals set out in the internationalisation strategy.

Due to the increasing number of foreign students and teachers, the increasing number of study programmes and courses offered in English, and the increasing number of publications in foreign journals and monographs, the use of English has expanded significantly. However, with the exception of scientific publications,

Table 3.1: Key Indicators of Internationalisation at UL in the Period 2014–2017

KEY INDICATORS OF INTERNATIONALISATION	2014	2017
No. of study programmes offered in English	17	62
No. of courses offered in English	444	496
No. of visiting teachers and researchers from abroad	387	591
No. of UL teachers and researchers being hosted by other universities	278	463
No. of foreign students enrolled at the UL	1,881	2,345
No. of incoming exchange students	1,411	2,026
No. of outgoing exchange students	1,130	1,130
No. of EU-financed research projects	437	444
No. of Web of Science registered publications	2,440	2,613
No. of UL publications' citations	268,453	398,304

internationalisation and the use of English remain quite limited in relative terms. The percentage of visiting teachers and researchers is about 15 % in comparison to the domestic ones, but they are seldom involved full-time. The number of study programmes offered in English is about 12 % out of all programmes, but the conditions for the implementation of teaching in English are not always met.

Despite the increasing internationalisation since 2014, the language strategy of the UL has not been elaborated and accepted. The working group to prepare the language strategy was established in 2017, a draft was made in 2018, but due to some changes in university management, the working group has not had a meeting since summer 2018. Does this mean that the use of Slovenian has been neglected, or is it just hard to define a strategy in circumstances of bipolarity between the defenders of the 'national interest' and the liberal views of those who believe that there is no need for the use of the national language in higher education and research?

Implementation of Language and Internationalisation Policies at the University of Ljubljana

As mentioned earlier in this chapter, the strategy of Slovenian and foreign language use has been elaborated on the national level in a rather general and vague form. It has been left to the universities to find concrete solutions in their daily practices and to stay within the legislative framework at the same time. However, universities have not made their language strategy explicit. Does this mean that the use of Slovene and foreign languages has been left completely to the choice of individual teachers and researchers? The answer is no, at least as far as the UL is concerned. There have been a number of measures accepted which try to balance between internationalisation and care for national identity, including the protection and development of Slovenian.

Slovenian is the language of communication and teaching at the UL. For its promotion, the Centre for Slovene language as a foreign language has long been in place. It offers courses of Slovenian to foreign staff and students and maintains the network of chairs of Slovenian language at over 60 foreign universities all around the world. About 3,000 students take part in the courses offered abroad every year. For internationalisation purposes the UL practises bilingualism (Slovene–English) in various situations. For instance, the university's website is available in both languages. Information about the UL addressed to potential and foreign students and to an international academic audience (booklets, leaflets, web journals…) is prepared in English. English is used at international conferences, research workshops, etc. in some situations with and in others without translation into Slovene or from Slovene to English.

Academic staff must meet certain language requirements:

- Slovenian candidates for employment at the UL must know at least one foreign language.
- Non-Slovenian teachers coming from abroad can start teaching in English as visiting professors. However, they must learn Slovenian if they want to stay at the university longer than three years.
- Courses of Slovenian are offered to foreign teachers and courses of English to Slovenian teachers. Where courses are offered to students in non-mother language it is important that teachers master the language they teach in.
- For academic promotion, teachers and researchers are required to publish in international journals, where in most cases non-Slovenian languages are used. In addition, everybody is obliged to publish a certain number of articles or other publications in Slovenian as well to prove that they care for the development of Slovenian terminology in their professional field.
- For academic promotion, Slovenian teachers and researchers are required to spend uninterruptedly at least three months at a foreign university or research institute.

For the promotion of multiculturalism and the balanced use of Slovenian and foreign (usually English) languages in the teaching process, the following provisions have been accepted at the UL:

- Foreign students who decide to be enrolled at the UL can use the so-called 'year+'. This means that in their first year at the UL, they mainly study the

Slovenian language and culture and must collect at least 30 credits in this way, and they can take subject courses as well. Later on they are able to continue their studies in Slovenian together with Slovenian students.

- Foreign students who stay at the UL for a shorter period—one to two semesters, mainly exchange students—are offered courses of Slovenian. They can learn some basics for everyday communication purposes. However, they cannot be expected to understand Slovenian as the medium of instruction for their university courses. Therefore, they are taught in foreign languages (i.e. mainly in English).
- Slovenian students are offered courses of foreign languages in most of the study programmes in order that they get acquainted with specific terminology in foreign languages and to be able to study literature and other sources written in foreign languages. The publication of textbooks in the Slovenian language to be used in the study process is promoted as well.
- A few study programmes are offered in English on the bachelor level, about a third on the master level and all of them on the doctoral level. Slovenian students can take part in these programmes as well. The same goes for quite a few courses that are offered in English on all three Bologna study levels.
- Foreign students are usually placed in mixed classes together with Slovenian students. Mixed classes are most desirable from the perspective of the Erasmus+ programme since they contribute to multiculturalism. In the mixed classes English is used in some cases: when the same programme/course/class is offered in parallel in Slovenian as well, when there is a bigger number (which is not precisely defined) of foreign students, when foreign teachers teach, or when Slovene students agree to teaching in English. If none of these conditions are met, foreign students are offered individual or small group tutorials in English by their teachers and fellow students.
- Students can write and defend their diploma and dissertation works in English if they have special reasons for it, such as being a foreign student, having a foreign professor as mentor, preparing their thesis abroad, being involved in an English track programme, etc. However, a long summary in Slovenian is required in this case. Works written in Slovenian must have summaries in English. The same rules apply for scientific publications published in Slovenia.

Discussion on Language Policy and its Implementation

Language policy in Slovenia has been elaborated on a general legislative level. In addition, resolutions on the national programme for language policy propose how to combine Slovenian language development and protection with internationalisation of higher education which requires the use of foreign languages in daily activities, research and study processes of universities. However, these documents do not elaborate language policies down to the implementation details. This is partially due to the autonomy left to the universities and particularly due to the polarisation of opinions where the majority wants a high protection of Slovenian and strict limits to the utilisation of foreign languages.

Whenever in the past a more detailed elaboration of measures was made and published, a discussion with conflicts arose and public campaigns against the use of foreign languages appeared. The situation resembles that of the other Southern European countries where high resistance against English has been observed (Hultgren, Jensen and Dimova 2015). One should rather opt for the Baltic approach:

> While the practices might still lean towards English as the dominant foreign language in the higher education context, there are distinct strategic steps taken in the institutional and national contexts to support maintaining cultural and linguistic diversity in Baltic states. (Tamtik and Young 2018)

Such an approach is particularly important in light of the fact that the spread of English in higher education is to a great extent a bottom-up process (Ferguson 2015) which needs a systematic counteraction from the state and universities to protect national languages and cultures.

At the University of Ljubljana, the situation seems to be worse, at least on the formal level. While one can find an explicit university internationalisation strategy document, a language strategy has not been elaborated yet. However, it is embodied in a number of partial and specific measures and remains on the level of a "hidden language policy" (Siiner 2010). This can be ascribed to the low level and high need for internationalisation and also to the split of opinions regarding the use of Slovenian and foreign languages at the university.

Perhaps the opportunity to elaborate a language strategy at the UL was missed when the internationalisation strategy was in preparation. Obviously, it was not realized in that moment that internationalisation and language policies are too often artificially insulated from each other (Gregersen et al., 2018) and that they should be considered as two sides of the same coin.

From a content point of view it seems that Slovenian language policy tends towards a cosmopolitan model (Kalin Golob et al., 2017) which is similar to the Nordic parallel use of the national and foreign languages (Gregersen et al., 2018). Both approaches see internationalisation which includes foreign language use as compatible with nurturing the national culture and language. The opening of a national culture to other cultures and exposure of a national language to other languages brings challenges that enhance cultural and linguistic development. With the appropriate national support—but not with total protection and isolation—culture and language can adjust to the changing domestic and global circumstances, increase their vitality and thus best serve to strengthen the national identity.

Taking into account the 11 recommendations on the use of local and international languages at universities set out by the Nordic Council (Gregersen et al., 2018), one can conclude that the UL follows all of them, even though its language policy has not been made explicit yet. At all these points there is also room for improvement: a language policy should be written down, the provisional language policy committee should become permanent, the language centre should be further developed offering additional services, more Slovenian language courses should be offered to foreign students and staff, administration should be offered more training in English, etc.

One of the burning issues is to what extent modern digital technology can help overcome the dilemmas concerning the use of national versus foreign languages. If there is not enough money and time for parallel classes or simultaneous translation by interpreters, will translation machines soon be sophisticated enough to efficiently step in? While machinery certainly can help in some situations, it is certain that the development of new terminology as a basis of machine programming will remain a responsibility of specialists in every specific area of science and the humanities. Last but not least, both human and technical solutions require additional resources if the nation wants universities to effectively care for internationalisation and its national identity.

Note

1. The text under this subtitle is based on the article published by Kalin Golob et al., 2017.

References

Accetto, Matej, 'Nacionalni jeziki, visoko šolstvo in mobilnost v pravu EU'. In Marjeta Humar and Mojca Žagar Karer, Eds, *Nacionalni jeziki v visokem* šolstvu; [National Languages in Higher Education] (Ljubljana: Založba SAZU, 2010), 25–35.

'The Act on Public Usage of Slovene', *The Official Gazette of the Republic of Slovenia* [no. 86 of *The Official Gazette of the Republic of Slovenia*] (Ljubljana: The Official Gazette of the Republic of Slovenia, 2004), 10114.

Dalmatin, Jurij, *Biblia* (Ljubljana: Narodna univerzitetna knjžnica, 1584).

De Wit, Hans, *Internationalisation of Higher Education in the United States of America and Europe: A Historical, Comparative and Conceptual Analysis* (Westport, Greenwood Press: 2002).

Fabricius, Anne, Janus Mortensen, and Hartmut Haberland, 'The Lure of Internationalisation: Paradoxical Discourses of International Student Mobility, Linguistic Diversity and Cross-cultural Exchange', *Higher Education* 73/4 (2017), 577–595.

Ferguson, Gibson, 'Introduction: Attitudes to English', in Andrew Linn, Neil Bermel, and Gibson Ferguson, eds, *Attitudes Towards English in Europe: English in Europe, Volume 1* (Berlin/Boston: Walter de Gruyter, 2015).

Gacel-Ávila, Jocelyne, 'The Internationalisation of Higher Education: A Paradigm for Global Citizenry', *Journal of Studies in International Education* 9 (2005), 121–136.

Gregersen, Frans, et al., *More parallel, please! Best Practice of Parallel Language at Nordic Universities: 11 recommendations* (Copenhagen: Nordic Council of Ministers, 2018).

Hultgren, Anna Kristina, Christian Jensen, and Slobodanka Dimova, 'English-Medium Instruction in European Higher Education: From the North to the South', in Slobodanka Dimova, Anna Kristina Hultgren, and Christian Jensen, eds, *English-Medium Instruction in European Higher Education. English in Europe No3* [vol. iii of *English in Europe*] (Berlin/Boston: Walter de Gruyter, 2015).

Kalin Golob, Monika, et al., 'Stayin' Alive? National Language and Internationalisation of Higher Education. The Case of Slovenia', *Croatian Journal of Education*, 19/4 (2017).

Kerr, Clark, 'The Internationalisation of Learning and the Nationalisation of the Purpose of Higher Education: The "Laws of Motion" in Conflict?', *European Journal of Education* 25/1 (1990), 5–22.

Knight, Jane, 'Internationalisation: Concepts, Complexities and Challenges', in James J.F.Forest and Philip G. Altbach, eds, *International Handbook of Higher Education* (Dordrecht: Springer, 2017), 207–227.

Ministrstvo za Izobraževanje, Znanost in Šport (MIZŠ), *Strategija internacionalizacije slovenskega visokega šolstva 2016–2020* [Strategy of Internationalisation of Slovenian Higher Education 2016 – 2020] (Ljubljana: Ministrstvo za Izobraževanje, Znanost in Šport, 2016), <https://www.cmepius.si/wp-content/uploads/2014/02/Strategija-internacionalizacije-slovenskega-visokega-solstva-SLO-2016 %E2 %80 %932020_WEB.pdf>.

Ministrstvo za Izobraževanje, Znanost in Šport (MIZŠ), *Higher Education Act* (Ljubljana: Ministrstvo za Izobraževanje, Znanost in Šport, 2019), <http://www.uradni-list.si/1/objava.jsp?urlid=201232&stevilka=1406>.

Ministrstvo za Kulturo (MK), *Resolution on the National Programme for Language Policy* (Ljubljana: Ministrstvo za Kulturo, 2015), <www.mk.gov.si/fileadmin/mk.gov.si/pageuploads/Ministrstvo/slovenski_jezik/Resolution_2014-18_Slovenia_jan_2015.pdf>.

Nokkala, Terhi, 'Constructing the Ideal University—The Internationalisation of Higher Education in the Competitive Knowledge Society', academic dissertation, University of Tampere, Tampere, 2007, <https://trepo.tuni.fi/bitstream/handle/10024/67779/978-951-44-7173-5.pdf?sequence=1&isAllowed=y>.

Perkin, Harold, 'History of Universities', in James J.F. Forest and Philip G. Altbach, eds, *International Handbook of Higher Education* (Dordrecht: Springer, 2017), 159–205.

Phillipson, Robert, 'English as Threat or Opportunity in European Higher Education', in Slobodanka Dimova, Anna Kristina Hultgren, and Christian Jensen, eds, *English-Medium Instruction in European Higher Education. English in Europe No3* [vol. iii of *English in Europe*] (Berlin/Boston: Walter de Gruyter, 2015).

Siiner, Maarja, 'Hangovers of Globalisation: A Case Study of Laisser-faire Language Policy in Denmark', *Language Policy and Language Planning* 34/1 (2010), 43–62.

Tamtik, Merli, and Soon Young Yang, 'Administering Higher Education Policies in the Baltic States: Balancing the Language Demands in Multilingual Society', *Journal of Multilingual and Multicultural Development* 39/9 (2018), 803–817.

'UL Home Page', UL Website, <http://www.uni-lj.si/eng/>.

Birute Klaas-Lang and Helle Metslang

Estonian in Higher Education: Challenges for a Medium-sized Language

In the higher-education space, which is open and international, universities are trying to keep a balance between teaching in the national language and international (i.e. almost always English-medium) teaching. The promotion of an international environment is important for universities from both a business and an institutional quality perspective. On the other hand, one of the missions of the university is to ensure the continuity of the native-language intelligentsia, which is needed for the continuation of the state and nationality and the development of one's mother tongue (in this case Estonian). The Estonian language, with its one million native speakers, is one of the least used languages in Europe with mother-tongue-medium higher education (including doctoral studies) and research. In this chapter, we will provide an overview of the language situation at Estonian universities, both in the past and present. We try to analyse the position of Estonian and English in Estonian higher education by observing language policies and strategies on a state and institutional level. This serves as an attempt to show how certain acts regulating the institutional language environment maintain a balance between higher education in the national language (in the case of a lesser-used language) and international openness.

Keywords: higher education, internationalisation, language policy, national language, universities, Estonia, Baltics

Introduction

In recent years, the question of the language of instruction in higher education has been an important topic in Estonia as well as in Europe as a whole. Studies on the internationalisation of higher education and the universities' choices of languages of instruction mainly point to the wide use of English as a *lingua franca* and emphasize the undeniably positive aspects of this tendency from the pragmatic point of view (Saarinen 2012; Risager 2012; Haberland and Mortensen 2012; Lindström 2012; Söderlundh 2012; Soler-Carbonell 2014; Soler 2019). Universities clearly need to offer English-taught curricula to international students which inevitably bring about the displacement of the native language as a language of instruction. The Nordic countries have attempted to reach a balance between the national language and English as the language of instruction by implementing parallel language use in language policy and in the practice of universities (Soler 2019, p. 8). Parallel language use should mean that the languages are used equally and simultaneously in instruction as well as in management. However, researchers point to problems in applying parallel language use in actual university life (Kuteeva 2014) and state outright that a "'parallel-linguistic framework' has the potential of creating more language barriers than it dissolves" (Fabricius et al., 2017).

While English is the indisputable leader on the "international education market" (Naidoo and Jamieson 2005), higher education has several important roles besides its market potential, such as preparing specialists needed by the society and the state and "providing a public service as national institutions" (Saarinen 2012, p. 158). In addition to the former, national language in higher education and research is a cultural phenomenon—a domain of language use that requires care and development.

Higher education and language policy analyses of Estonia as well as other Baltic countries indicate that in the globalizing world the internationalisation of universities is swift in this region and has brought about a noticeable increase in the relative importance of English as a language of instruction (cf. Klaas-Lang 2012; Soler and Vihman 2017; Selliov 2017; Rozenvalde 2018; Soler 2019). However, English as a language of instruction does not accompany the national language but frequently replaces it as is evident in the empirics of the current chapter. It is therefore necessary to analyse the sustainability of languages with a relatively small number of speakers in a situation where the domains of language use are starting to narrow.

While the discourse of the sustainability of languages originally concentrated on minority languages, by now it has transferred to languages with a considerably larger number of native speakers. Such a broadening of the approach was mainly caused by the need to ensure linguistic diversity in renewed language environments and in the sociolinguistic situation that has been brought about by globalisation and changes in modern society (cf. Ehala 2010; Soler-Carbonell 2012; Ehala et al., 2014).

Contemporary society is characterized by a global exchange of information as well as migration, which have greatly influenced the intensity of language contacts, but also changed their nature. There are no state borders in the virtual world, and the virtual environment provides many choices for the language user as well as opportunities to withdraw from the native language space. Thus, even the status of the official or state language and the existence of supporting infrastructure do not guarantee a future for a language since the use of English has expanded exponentially in education and commerce as well as in economics (Vertovec 2007, 2010). The possible impact of this side effect of globalisation, i.e. of the globalisation of English, on the sustainability of languages has been widely recognized (Skutnabb-Kangas 2000; Phillipson 2003, 2009; Hagege 2006; Canagarajah 2007). Several research-based national language programmes and strategies also exist (e.g. in Sweden, Estonia, Finland), created in order to ensure the continuation of the functions of the official language in all domains of life (Mål i mun 2002; DSEL 2004; DPEL 2011; Hakulinen et al., 2009).

The language of higher education has been emphasized as one of the most important indicators among the factors of language sustainability (cf. Soler-Carbonell 2012; Vilà and Bretxa 2014). There is every reason to agree with David Crystal (2002, p. 13) when he claims that even a language spoken by 20 million people could be called a disabled language if the dominant language in higher education is English.

National languages being replaced by English in their former functions in one domain (higher education and research) can first cause a loss in an adjacent domain (e.g. general education), followed by further loss elsewhere. The study on 'The State of Language in Estonia' compiled in 2017 points out, based on interviews with experts, that language use in higher education and research is often the most fragile and vulnerable area, "since it influences students' communication skills as well as the functionality of Estonian in every domain. Language use in higher education is therefore one of the pivotal parameters and influencing factors of language vitality" (Lukk et al., 2017, p. 45).

EFNIL (European Federation of National Institutions for Language[1]), an organisation uniting the councils and institutions of official languages in Europe, dedicated their annual conference in 2014 in Florence and the volume published in 2015 entitled *Language Use in University Teaching and Research* (Stickel and Robustelli 2015) to the language of higher education and research. At the conference in Florence, linguists from 30 countries also approved a resolution concerning the language use of university teaching and research (Stickel and Robustelli 2015, p. 290), which

> regards the current tendency towards the use of English as a language of academic instruction in non-Anglophone countries with deep concern. This tendency to use English instead of the standard languages of the various countries in university teaching and research restricts the domains of these languages and their development and thus endangers the linguistic diversity of Europe that is essential for the cultural diversity and wealth of our continent.

EFNIL also communicated an urgent recommendation to the academic and political authorities of non-Anglophone countries to "encourage teachers and students to use their respective national languages for research and studies" (Stickel and Robustelli 2015, p. 291).

In Estonia, too, politicians together with experts have repeatedly discussed the topics related to the language policy of the state-funded higher education. The discussions have also reached the level of parliament and thus, in 2017, the Estonian Parliament had a discussion 'Is Estonian-instructed higher education on the verge of extinction?'[2] In continuation of this, the Estonian Parliament discussed the issue of the sustainability of the Estonian language in key domains—general education and higher education—as an issue of national importance.[3]

The present chapter gives an overview of the position of Estonian in higher education, continuing the authors' previous research on the topic of the language of higher education in the framework of language sustainability (Klaas-Lang 2012, 2014a, 2014b, 2016; Klaas-Lang and Metslang 2015, 2018). The data originates from documents concerning Estonian higher education and language policy, but also from a data set collected with the help of the Ministry of Education and Research and colleagues from the University of Tartu.[4] The authors also make use of their extensive experience working as professors at the University of Tartu and the University of Helsinki and as compilers of the Estonian Language Council language policy strategies.

The Language Environment in Estonia: Sociolinguistic Background

According to Statistics Estonia the population of Estonia on 1 January 2019 was 1,323,824.[5] By the size of its population, Estonia is one of the smallest countries in Europe, 14 times smaller than what could be called the average European Union country. The population has been decreasing since 1989 due to emigration and low birth rate, and the decrease is greater among non-Estonian residents than among Estonian residents (EHDR 2008, p. 48). However, recent years have seen a deceleration of emigration and from 2015 onwards Estonia has been an immigration country instead of an emigration country.

According to the 2011 census there are representatives of 192 nations living in Estonia: 68.7 % of the resident population are Estonian (889,770), 24.8 % are Russian (321,198) and 1.7 % are Ukrainian (22,302). The proportion of Belorussians (12,419) and Finns (7,423) remains below 1 %. Compared to the 2000 census the number of Estonians has increased by 1 % and the number of Russians decreased by the same amount.

There are 157 languages spoken as a mother tongue in Estonia. Over the past ten years, Estonia has become considerably more multilingual, since the previous census registered 109 languages spoken as mother tongue. The most widely spoken mother tongues are Estonian (886,859; 68.5 %), Russian (383,062; 29.6 %) and Ukrainian (8,012; 0.6 %).

The Estonian language skills of non-Estonians have started to improve consistently in recent years. Studies conducted so far show that the proportion of 15–74-year-old non-Estonians claiming to have at least passive knowledge of Estonian has more than doubled in the last couple of decades: from 34 % (1997) to 85 % (2017).[6] The analysis of statistical data still shows that there is a considerable number of people in Estonia whose knowledge of the official language is not sufficient for their social and professional life.[7]

Higher Education in Estonia

Historical Overview

The beginnings of higher education in Estonia reach back to 1632 when the Swedish king Gustav II Adolf established the first university in Tartu—*Academia Gustaviana*. The language of instruction, as everywhere in Europe at that time, was Latin. However, due to wars the provision of higher education in Estonia was shortly interrupted, and it was not until 1802 that the University of Tartu was reopened under the name of *Kaiserliche Universität zu Dorpat*, with German as the language of instruction. Estonia belonged to the Tsardom of Russia but German retained its position as the official language and language of education for some time, along with the privileges of the Baltic German estate owners. Estonian reached the university as a subject in 1803 when Friedrich David Lenz first started his lectures introducing the Estonian language (Klaas 2003, p. 319). The language of instruction was changed to Russian only in the last decade of the nineteenth century, specifically in 1895, together with a change of the name of the university to *Imperatorskij Jur'evskij Universitet*. The independence of the Estonian state, achieved in 1918, also led the way to the emergence of Estonian-language higher education: on 1 December 1919 the University of Tartu of the Estonian Republic was opened. The first years contained plenty of teaching in foreign languages since the majority of the professors could not speak Estonian. However, in about ten years the University of Tartu transformed from being *de jure* Estonian speaking to being *de facto* Estonian speaking: foreign professors learned Estonian and a new generation of native Estonian professors became available.

Estonian-language higher education has therefore been possible for the last hundred years and was not interrupted even during the Soviet occupation. Admittedly, from 1944 to 1989 more and more Russian-language programmes were created alongside the Estonian-language ones in the University of Tartu as well as other Estonian higher education institutions, and from 1975 all doctoral dissertations presented for defense had to be written in Russian. However, Estonian remained the main language of instruction of higher education in Estonia even during the Soviet occupation.

Current Situation

In the academic year 2018–19, there were a total of 20 institutions of higher education in Estonia: six public universities and one private university, eight state and five private institutions of professional higher education, with a total of 45,815 students.[8] The University of Tartu (UT) is the only classical *universitas*-type university that provides programmes in all fields of study, including medicine. The other universities in Estonia are Tallinn University (TU), Tallinn University of Technology (TalTech), Estonian University of Life Sciences (EULS), Estonian Academy of Arts (EAA), Estonian Academy of Music and Theatre (EAMT), and Estonian Business School (EBS). The last-mentioned is a private university, the rest are public universities. While only a couple of years ago there were almost 70,000 university students in Estonia, this indicator has decreased considerably due to the demographic situation in Estonia (see Table 4.1 in the section 'Language of Instruction'). Universities and institutions of professional higher education offer programmes in Estonian, Russian and English. The language of instruction in higher education has been Estonian since 1919, when after Estonia became independent the University of Tartu started teaching in Estonian. According to the Universities Act (UA, article 22(8)) and the Institutions of Professional Higher Education Act (IPHEA, article 17) the language of instruction at universities and institutions of professional higher education is Estonian; the use of other languages shall be decided by the council of the institution (public and private universities) or the Minister of Education and Research (public institutions of higher education). In addition to state-financed study places the institutions of higher education can admit students who finance their own studies. The higher education reform of 2013 created a connection between the language of instruction and funding under the banner of free Estonian-language higher education: the state shall finance programmes where the language of instruction is Estonian; paid study places can only be created for foreign-language curricula (AA 2012).

The Legal Space of Estonian and Language Policy Strategies

For a language to function successfully, its legal space must be ensured and regulated. Estonian is the official language of Estonia according to the Language Act of 1989 and its more current versions. It is extremely noteworthy that the first Language Act was already adopted before Estonia regained its independence. It was called 'The Language Act of the Estonian Soviet Socialist Republic' and stated in article 60 that

> the official language of the Estonian Soviet Socialist Republic is Estonian. In Estonia, the indigenous habitat of Estonians, the Estonian language is under special observation and protection of the state. By legalizing Estonian as the official language a strong basis has been established for the preservation and development of the Estonian nation and its culture. (Language Act 1989)

On 23 February 2011, the Parliament adopted a renewed Language Act whose purpose (as the purpose of the previous Language Act and its amendments) was "to develop, preserve and protect the Estonian language and ensure the use of the Estonian language as the main language for communication in all spheres of public life" (Language Act 2011).[9] The new Language Act also provides that "the official language of Estonia is Estonian" (Language Act 2011).[10]

The legal protection of the Estonian language has found its way into the Constitution (Estonian Constitution 2011), according to which the state must ensure the preservation of the Estonian nation, language and culture through times: article 6 of the Constitution states that the official language of Estonia is Estonian. It is the state's duty to ensure everyone's right to be taught in Estonian (article 37), everyone's right to conduct their business and communicate with government agencies and local authorities in Estonian (article 51), and the use of Estonian by government agencies and local authorities (article 52). In order to ensure the rights granted to Estonian by legal regulations, the state, primarily via the Language Inspectorate, also engages in the protection of the language.[11]

For over 20 years, the state of Estonia has contributed to the strategic planning of the language domain. On 21 April 1998, the Government recorded a decision by which it assigned the Ministry of Education (now Ministry of Education and Research) the task to create a strategy for developing the Estonian language. On 6 April 2000, by the order of the Minister of Education, an Estonian organizing committee for the European Year of Languages (later renamed the Estonian Language Council) was established, with one of its tasks being the creation of the aforementioned strategy, but also advising the Government in the questions of language policy as provided by its statutes: "The Estonian Language Council consults the Government of Estonia on the development and execution of the language policy" (Language Act 2011).[12] On 5 August 2004 the Government approved the 'Development Strategy of the Estonian Language 2004–2010' (DSEL 2004) and on 25 November 2010 the 'The Development Plan of the Estonian Language 2011–2017' (DPEL 2011) and its implementation plan, which was compiled by the Ministry of Education and Research in cooperation with the Estonian Language Council. The development plan proposed 13 measures for the development of the Estonian language, in order to ensure the functioning of Estonian as an official language in all spheres of life, its development capacity and its status as the common language of communication among the population of Estonia. The development plan included topics on language management (general language, language service provider, and name management), the study of Estonian, language resources, language-technological support of the Estonian language, education and Estonian-language instruction (general education in Estonian, Estonian in non-Estonian-medium general education, vocational education, higher education), varieties of the Estonian language (regional varieties, Estonian as used by Estonians living abroad, sign language and language use by people with special linguistic needs), Estonian in the multilingual world, the supervision of the observance of the Language Act and awareness-raising activities with regards to language.

Alas, there was no follow-up to the last development plan, mainly due to political differences, but also due to a different view of the broadness of the development plan's goals and activities by language experts and the officials of the ministry (cf. Klaas-Lang 2017; ÕPLeht 2018). The Estonian Language Council as a broad-based expert group also ceased its activity in the end of 2016. A new council was formed, although with significantly fewer members and significantly smaller visibility in the society. Whether the reduced membership and being under the authority of the language department of the Ministry of Education and Research will lead to changes in the state's language policy remains to be seen in the near future.

At the time of writing this chapter (April 2019), there is an agreement that the Ministry of Education and Research will prepare a vision paper 'The Basic Principles of Estonian Language Policy', which should be completed during this year and which could be used for creating a new language strategy.[13]

In the domain of higher education, the previous development plan had the objective that

> Estonian-medium higher education ensuring a high level of Estonian-language proficiency among graduates of institutions of higher education will be available on all levels of study in all groups of programmes, whereas opportunities of instruction in foreign languages will be supported, too; major research results will also be published in

> Estonian, thus preserving and developing the Estonian language of science and avoiding a complete transition to a foreign language in any branch of science. (DPEL 2011)

In order to support Estonian-language higher education and research, several state-funded programmes have also been initiated.[14] These programmes continue the successful activities of the previous funding period in the fields of language technology, research development, terminology and publishing textbooks for higher education institutions: (1) Estonian Language Technology 2018–2027 (previous programmes for 2006–10 and 2011–17), (2) Estonian terminology work 2018–2021, development via the Language programme (previous programmes for 2008–12 and 2013–17) and (3) Estonian-language textbooks for higher education institutions 2018–2027 (previous programmes for 2008–12 and 2013–17).[15,16,17] In summer 2019 the programme for supporting research and development of Estonian language will start (previous programmes for 2009–13 and 2014–18).[18]

The Legal Space of Estonian Higher Education and the Estonian Language

The legal space of higher education in Estonia is regulated by the Universities Act and the Institutions of Professional Higher Education Act. Both acts legalize the use of Estonian as the language of instruction and regulate the use of other languages in higher education: "the language of instruction at universities is Estonian. The use of other languages shall be decided by the council of a university" (UA); "the language of instruction at institutions of professional higher education is Estonian. The use of other languages is decided by the minister who directs the ministry under whose area of government the particular institution of professional higher education belongs" (IPHEA). During the time that these acts were established the important development priorities and options for higher education were written down in two strategic documents which both emphasized the position and development of the Estonian language. The language of instruction in higher education was mentioned in the 'Estonian Higher Education Strategy 2006–2015', where one of the objectives was

> to ensure the development of Estonian-medium educational and cultural space. Ensure the continuation and development of Estonian-medium higher education in the European open education space. The objective is for Estonian-medium higher education to be available in all fields and on all levels of study. (EHES)

The Estonian Higher Education Internationalisation Strategy 2006–2015 emphasized the importance of higher education internationalisation and thus the need to develop English-medium curricula. The strategy also mentioned the important role of the universities with respect to the development of the official language and determined very clearly the role of Estonian as the language of instruction: “while opening Estonian higher education and bringing an international dimension into each curriculum we must ensure the preservation of Estonian as the primary language of instruction and research in institutions of higher education” (EHEIS). The period of validity for both aforementioned documents has ended and the most important guidelines for Estonian higher education can now be found in ‘The Estonian Lifelong Learning Strategy 2020’ and the implementation plan based on its guidelines and visions ‘Higher Education Programme (2016–2019)’.[19,20] The Lifelong Learning Strategy addresses the education opportunities of students with mother tongues other than Estonian and the ensuring of the teaching of Estonian to all age groups. However, the preservation and development of Estonian-medium higher education—the domain of language use important for the sustainability of language—is not mentioned. The higher education programme pays much attention to internationalisation and foreign language learning but maintaining the position of Estonian as a language of higher education is not named here either. Looking at the changes in the national higher education policy in the past ten years, one sees an obvious tendency to emphasize the need for internationalisation and for institutions of higher education to become foreign language medium as guarantees of academic success and quality. While the state finances the development of Estonian special language vocabulary and the compiling and publishing of Estonian-language textbooks for institutions of higher education, without Estonian-speaking users these textbooks will remain to gather dust on the shelf and the special language vocabulary will not have a chance to be entrenched in the language.

Preservation and Development of Mother-tongue-medium Higher Education in Political Debates

In March 2019, Estonia elected the Parliament (*Riigikogu*) and unlike previously, during these elections the language issues held a prominent position in the parties’ manifestos, mainly with regard to the language of instruction at general education schools, but also in institutions of higher education.[21] From the point of view of this chapter, it is important to analyse to which extent the larger parties in Estonia pay attention to the language policy of higher education. After all, the manifestos reflect debates that are also ongoing in society. Estonian as a language of higher education, especially in the context of internationalisation and demographic processes, has received a great deal of attention in the manifestos. Does being an Estonian university mean that the primary language of instruction on the bachelor's and master's level is Estonian? The Estonian centrist party Keskerakond does not give a straightforward answer to this question but emphasizes the need "to develop Estonian-medium study materials for institutions of higher education, to support the teaching of Estonian in schools abroad and research activity related to the development of the Estonian language".[22] All the activities mentioned are very important but they do not answer the main question that the public cares about: will the Estonian university remain Estonian-medium? A new player on the Estonian political field, Eesti 200 [Estonia 200], who identify themselves as a new force consisting of experts searching for the Estonian vision for the future, dedicate considerably more space to the higher education language policy than Keskerakond, but mainly in the context of paid higher education, supporting the broadening of English-medium education while providing foreign students more instruction on the Estonian language and society. However, on balance, they admit that "for the development of the language it is very important to also actively use the more complicated Estonian language of research".[23]

On the whole, the parties are rather cautious about the requirement of preserving Estonian as the language of instruction in higher education, recognizing the importance of Estonian-medium higher education and the development of the language of research for the Estonian state but mainly concentrating on digital solutions and the development of terminology. In the opinion of several parties, speech recognition and machine translation should also solve the language problems of higher education. Nonetheless, the manifesto of the Social Democratic Party states without prevarication: "Estonian public institutions of higher education must provide free Estonian-medium education in all specialties."[24] There is no specification as to on which academic level and to what extent, but all of the other parties neglect such details as well, with the exception of the conservative Isamaa who, in addition to their general statement "we consider important Estonian-medium teaching in higher education and the development of Estonian language of research", also have a requirement for all doctoral dissertations to be in Estonian.[25] Isamaa connects the state funding of the universities to Estonian-medium teaching: "In financing institutions of higher education we prefer Estonian-medium curricula by financing institutions of higher education through state-commissioned study places, we will restrict the cross-subsidizing and subsidizing of foreign-language-medium curricula." Vabaerakond, who in 2018 initiated the discussion on the position of the Estonian language as the language of instruction in higher education in the Parliament, have also mentioned this issue in their manifesto: "We support the internationalisation of universities, but not at the expense of the Estonian language and culture"[26]. They are promising to direct the state funding of the universities "mainly towards the Estonian-medium curricula".[27] According to the liberal Reform Party, foreign students should be more integrated into Estonian life in the future: "We consider the continuation and strengthening of Estonian-medium higher education important. We therefore deem it necessary to develop Estonian-medium curricula and to add study modules of Estonian language, culture and society to all English-medium curricula."[28]

In addition to the language of instruction, the working language of higher education is also becoming a topic of discussion: to what extent does the state want Estonian universities to work in Estonian? Isamaa indicates the need to preserve Estonian as the working language at institutions of higher education and considers it necessary for "visiting faculty who remain in Estonia for a longer time to learn Estonian."

By the time this chapter was written (April 2019) the elections were over and the coalition in Estonia had been formed between conservative parties led by the centrists. Which parts of the parties' manifestos have reached the coalition contract (Coalition Contract 2019)? There is a rather generally worded agreement that the proportion of Estonian-medium higher education must not decrease and that it has to be free for the students. The contract does not preclude foreign-language-medium (i.e. English-medium) curricula which should be paid for and connected with various international cooperation programmes. Compared to the pre-election positions the education policy of the coalition contract is considerably more moderate and general. However, the decision to stop the decrease of the proportion of Estonian-medium higher education included in the contract can be considered important for the preservation of the domains of use of the Estonian language. It is especially notable that for the first time the ensuring of the sustainability of Estonian in higher education has reached the level of government principles (cf. Coalition Contract 2016; Coalition Contract 2015). The previous government principles have had the objective of internationalizing higher education. For instance, the Coalition Contract of 2015 emphasized the need to support "the internationalisation of the universities and the increasing of the proportion of visiting faculty as well as foreign students."

The Situation of Language Use in Estonian Higher Education

Language of Instruction

Next, we will address the role of persons with different languages and different linguistic backgrounds in Estonian higher education based on the data from the Estonian Educational Information System (EEIS), the reports on the Development Plan for the Estonian Language (IDPEL 2013; IDPEL 2015), and data collected from institutions of higher education.

Estonian is the primary language of instruction on all levels of education as it was two decades ago (see Table 4.1). Compared to the time after Estonia regained its independence, the proportion of students studying in Russian has decreased considerably while the proportion of students studying in English has increased. On the one hand, the high percentage of Russian-medium studies in the 1990s was based on the existence of Russian-medium study groups that were left from the time of the Soviet Union, but on the other hand, the liberal capitalist way of life created opportunities to establish new educational institutions, and the opportunities were widely used. Relatively small universities and institutions of professional higher education, many of which catered for Russian-speaking students in particular, were established. However, the state later started to verify whether the education provided in institutions of higher education adhered to the required quality standards and many private educational institutions had to close down causing a drastic decrease in the amount of Russian-medium education. The proportion of English-medium education, on the contrary, has been increasing steadily. The proportion of students studying in Russian decreased from 17 % to 2 % during 1993–2013 and has remained on that level to this day. The proportion of students studying in English has on the contrary increased from 2 % to 12 % since 2012. The proportion of students studying in Estonian initially showed a significant increase (82 % in 1993, 91 % in 2012) but then began to drop consistently. The current level (81 %) is lower than in 1993. Curricula of doctoral studies, for which designating two languages is allowed, are predominantly Estonian- and English-medium.

The higher education reform, started in 2013, has undoubtedly influenced the shifts in recent years. Institutions of higher education have been compensated for the loss of paid Estonian-medium education by the state but they have also taken steps to gain sources of income in the form of tuition fees by establishing foreign-language-medium curricula. Examples of English-medium curricula opened or turned into paid curricula include the master's programmes of E-governance technologies and technology of wood and plastics at the Tallinn University of Technology, medicine at the University of Tartu, and veterinary medicine at the Estonian University of Life Sciences. The programmes are targeted at foreign students (including the Finns who have thus far studied on paid study places in Estonian due to the similarity of Estonian and Finnish, especially medicine and veterinary medicine) and also Estonian students. With the broadening of English-medium studies, the number of foreign students has rapidly increased

Table 4.1: Distribution of University Students Between Languages of Instruction 1993 and 2012–2018[29]

LANGUAGE OF INSTRUCTION	1993		2012		2013		2014		2015		2016		2017		2018	
Estonian	20,585	82 %	61,496	91 %	53,009	88 %	47,738	87 %	42,835	84 %	39,474	83 %	37,529	81 %	36,941	81 %
English	176	1 %	1,642	2 %	3,248	5 %	3,899	7 %	4,439	9 %	4,858	10 %	5,635	12 %	5,792	13 %
Russian	4,303	17 %	4,469	7 %	1,425	2 %	1,246	2 %	1,096	2 %	909	2 %	857	2 %	746	2 %
Total	25,064		67,607		59,998		55,214		51,092		47,794		46,155		45,815	

(1,874 in 2012; 4,394 in 2017; 5,047 in 2018). By this indicator, in the academic year 2016–17, Estonia with its 10 % of foreign students was 'more international' than for example Finland, where the proportion of foreign students in the given year was 7.7 %. In the academic year of 2018–19 the proportion of foreign students is already 11.0 %.

The distribution of curricula between languages of instruction in Estonian institutions of higher education is summarized in Tables 4.2, 4.3, and 4.4. It can be seen that English-medium curricula together with Estonian- and English-medium curricula constitute 25 % of all curricula in the academic year 2018–19 (the proportion was as high as 30 % in the previous academic year). Simultaneously, the students enrolled in these curricula constitute 18 % (17 % in the previous academic year) of the total number of students (13 % of students study in English, 5 % in Estonian and English). Thus, relatively speaking, there are fewer students per curriculum for the English-medium curricula than for the Estonian-medium curricula. This raises a question: does the small number of students in the English-medium curricula ensure the profitability of the programmes or is English-medium education financed at the expense of Estonian-medium education?

This difference is mainly caused by the fact that the English-medium curricula can be found primarily on the second and third level of education: the English-medium curricula are predominantly master's programmes and doctoral programmes with Estonian and English as languages of instruction (see Table 4.4). For the latter, the Estonian language ensures the funding and the English language ensures the international dimension of the research. On the bachelor's level the curricula are predominantly Estonian-medium. In Estonian-medium curricula, English is used in individual subjects and modules, and some of the reading materials are also in English. This tendency towards the division of the functions of language between different levels of higher education is present in all fields and is consistent with observations in other countries. The increase in the percentage of English-medium master's programmes in Estonia has been rapid: in autumn 2012 9 % of all curricula were English-medium, in 2014 the proportion was 21 % and by now we have reached a level of 38 %.

The number of active curricula in Estonia has been decreased considerably to prevent the steadily decreasing number of students from being divided among many costly curricula: last year students were enrolled in 838 curricula, this year in 703 curricula. The overall picture has therefore slightly improved: the proportion of Estonian-medium curricula has increased and the division of the students enrolled in the English-medium curricula has decreased. The increase in the number of English-medium curricula has also lessened, possibly also due

Table 4.2: Distribution of Curricula Between Languages of Instruction 2013–2019 (Absolute Numbers)

LANGUAGE OF THE CURRICULUM	2013–14	2014–15	2015–16	2016–17	2017–18	2018–19
Estonian and English (doctoral study)	121	136	142	144	137	69
Estonian and Russian (doctoral study)	3	3	3	4	4	1
Estonian	666	628	611	599	561	514
English	90	94	106	125	115	102
Russian	29	30	35	30	21	17
Total	**909**	**891**	**897**	**902**	**838**	**703**

Table 4.3: Distribution of Curricula Between the Main Languages of Instruction 2013–2019 (Percentage of Total Number of Curricula)

LANGUAGE OF THE CURRICULUM	2013–14	2014–15	2015–16	2016–17	2017–18	2018–19
Estonian and English (doctoral study)	13 %	15 %	16 %	16 %	16 %	10 %
Estonian	73 %	70 %	68 %	66 %	67 %	73 %
English	10 %	11 %	12 %	14 %	14 %	15 %
Russian	3 %	3 %	4 %	3 %	3 %	2 %

to achieving and surpassing the goal of the internationalisation of higher education (10 % of English-medium curricula) and the public pressure to support Estonian as a language of higher education.

According to the Development Plan for the Estonian Language (DPEL 2011), the previous Developing Strategy of the Estonian Language (DSEL 2014) and the draft of the next development strategy (DSELD 2017), Estonian-medium studies must be preserved in all specialties. We consider the detailed fields in the ISCED classification of education and training to be equivalent to specialties (UNESCO 2018, 2019).[31] DPEL (2011) included among its objectives the preservation of Estonian-medium higher education in all detailed fields on all levels of education. In broad terms, the planned level has been retained. The data for 2012, 2013 and 2014 show that all detailed fields contained Estonian-medium curricula on all levels of education. The developments of the last couple of years have nonetheless endangered the above-mentioned principle; in the academic year 2018–19

Table 4.4: The Languages of the Curricula of Bachelor's, Master's, and Doctoral Studies 2013–2019

LEVEL	ESTONIAN AND ENGLISH	ESTONIAN AND RUSSIAN	ESTONIAN	ENGLISH	RUSSIAN	TOTAL
2013–14						
Bachelor's			190	22	3	215
Master's			270	62	5	337
Doctoral	121	3	15	2		141
Total curricula[30]	**121**	**3**	**666**	**90**	**29**	**909**
2014–15						
Bachelor's			180	20	2	202
Master's			251	67	5	323
Doctoral	136	3	15	2		156
Total curricula	**136**	**3**	**628**	**94**	**30**	**891**
2015–16						
Bachelor's			181	20	3	204
Master's			241	74	7	322
Doctoral	142	3	3	2		150
Total curricula	**142**	**3**	**611**	**106**	**35**	**897**
2016–17						
Bachelor's			191	23	2	216
Master's			231	87	4	322
Doctoral	144	4	1	2		151
Total curricula	**144**	**4**	**599**	**125**	**30**	**902**
2017–18						
Bachelor's			185	20	1	206
Master's			219	80	3	302

(*continued on next page*)

Table 4.4: (continued)

LEVEL	ESTONIAN AND ENGLISH	ESTONIAN AND RUSSIAN	ESTONIAN	ENGLISH	RUSSIAN	TOTAL
Doctoral	137	4	2	1		144
Total curricula	**137**	**4**	**561**	**115**	**21**	**838**
2018–2019						
Bachelor's			173	16		190
Master's			194	73	2	269
Doctoral	69	1	1	1		72
Total curricula	**69**	**1**	**514**	**102**	**17**	**703**

there are nine detailed fields which do not have Estonian-medium curricula on the master's level. Admittedly, all these detailed fields are small (containing 1–2 curricula) and for the most part Estonian-medium curricula exist in the same detailed field on another level of education. For instance, the detailed field for the interdisciplinary programmes and qualifications involving arts and humanities contains one Estonian- and English-medium doctoral curriculum, while the only master's programme here is the programme for literature, visual culture and film studies opened in 2017 (TU). The narrow field of 'Information and Communication Technologies' (ICTs) only has an English-medium master's programme in the detailed field 'Database and network design and administration' (the cyber security programme, TalTech) and in the detailed field of 'Information and Communication Technologies' not elsewhere classified (E-governance technologies and services, TU). In the case of the other specialties discussed here, related specialties are available in the Estonian language on other academic levels. The specialty of E-governance, however, has no Estonian support on other academic levels. Master's programmes solely in English exist also in the detailed fields of 'Materials' (glass, paper, plastic and wood) and 'Mechanics and metal trades' (all programmes in TalTech). For doctoral studies, the overwhelming majority of curricula in all detailed fields have two languages of instruction, Estonian and English.

Estonian-medium education requires Estonian-medium study materials and terminology. Both elements are being pursued actively and have also been supported by the state in the form of relevant programmes, and in addition, each year the authors of the best textbooks for institutions of higher education are rewarded.

The Language of Publication of Study and Research Results

According to the standard of higher education the student must

> be able to explain the issues related to his or her specialty in speech and writing and to participate in professional debates in the language of instruction and at least one foreign language in order to be awarded the Bachelor's degree and a diploma. (SHE 2008)

In order to receive a master's degree the student must

> be able to present and discuss the problems related to his or her specialty, the conclusions and the theories on which these are based in speech and writing and to participate in relevant discussions with experts as well as laymen in the language of instruction and a foreign language that is important for his or her specialty. (SHE 2008)

To receive a doctoral degree the student must

> be able to present the problems, conclusions and the theories on which these are based, related to his or her field of study and his or her dissertation in speech and writing to an

> audience of experts in the field, in communication with laymen, to argue and participate in relevant debates in the language of instruction and in a foreign language important in that field, as well as publish original research results in peer-reviewed publications or in art specialties publish creative works to an international audience. (SHE 2008)

The requirements set for the final papers of different levels are regulated by the institutions of higher education themselves but these are generally written in the language of instruction or another language that is important in the field and a resume is added to the paper, in a foreign language for a paper written in Estonian and *vice versa*. The agreements between the rectors of Estonian universities signed in 2003 and 2006 include the valuing and developing of the Estonian language of research. The tasks and outcomes of doctoral studies emphasize the necessity to use a foreign language: one of the objectives is to develop further the ability to express oneself in one's field of study in writing and speech in at least one foreign language. Similarly, the mandatory components of doctoral studies include part-time study in a foreign language at the home university, and one of the skills that should be obtained through doctoral studies is to write an academic article as well as to teach and instruct in both one's mother tongue and a foreign language. An agreement has been reached regarding doctoral dissertations:

> A Doctoral dissertation includes a resume containing the objectives, methods and results of the research, which is in Estonian in case of a dissertation written in a foreign language and in a foreign language in case of a dissertation written in Estonian. (ECR)

No agreement has been reached as to the extent of the resume although the Development Plan for the Estonian Language (DPEL) already stipulated a comprehensive resume of the length of an academic article in the field. The regulations of universities do not generally determine the length of the resume. The lengthier resumes can be found in the dissertations of EAA, EBS and UT. Developing the Estonian language of research through doctoral dissertations is most problematic in the field of engineering since, with one exception, all dissertations defended in TalTech in the period of 2013–18 are written in a foreign language with the required length of the resume being 1–2 pages. In reality, the Estonian resume of a foreign-language (predominantly English-language) dissertation is considered a formality in many universities. The majority of doctoral dissertations are written in English, but there are also some dissertations in Russian, German and Finnish. Dissertations in Estonian are more common in the humanities and arts and in law. To motivate the quality of the Estonian resumes of dissertations a prize for the best Estonian resume of the year was founded. An overview of the languages of the dissertations defended by university is presented in Table 4.5.

Table 4.5: The Languages of Dissertations 2013–2018

	2013 Estonian	**2013 Foreign language**	**2014 Estonian**	**2014 Foreign language**	**2015 Estonian**	**2015 Foreign language**	**2016 Estonian**	**2016 Foreign language**	**2017 Estonian**	**2017 Foreign language**	**2018 Estonian**	**2018 Foreign language**
UT	17	99	11	98	12	101	9	110	15	130	19	110
TalTech	0	54	0	57	0	61	0	74	0	62	1	76
EULS	0	14	0	18	0	13	0	20	0	18	0	9
TU	11	12	6	8	7	18	3	16	7	15	4	18
EBS	0	3	1	1	1	1	0	2	0	1	0	3
EAA	1	2	1	1	0	2	2	1	2	1	0	2
EAMT	2	1	2	1	1	3	3	2	4	1	1	1
Total	31	185	21	184	21	199	17	225	28	228	25	219
Percentage	14,4 %	85,6 %	10,2 %	89,8 %	9,5 %	90,5 %	7,0 %	93,0 %	10,9 %	89,1 %	10,2 %	89,8 %

Academic publications, especially in the fields of sciences, engineering, life sciences and medicine are also predominantly written in English. Yet, as of April 2019, there are 11 academic journals from the fields of the humanities, social sciences and medicine belonging to the highest bibliometric category (1.1) of the Estonian Research Information System (ERIS) that publish articles in Estonian, for example *Keel ja Kirjandus, Methis, Mäetagused, Kunstiteaduslikke Uurimusi, Usuteaduslik Ajakiri, Acta Historica Tallinnensia, Halduskultuur, Eesti Arst*. Thus, the position of Estonian has improved somewhat, as in 2017 there were eight such journals.

Attention has also been paid to awareness-raising with regard to research, mainly aimed at Estonian target groups and supporting Estonian as a research language. Annual competitions of student papers and studies are being organized, national research awards are issued, there are competitions of popularizing science, research-themed series in TV, radio and printed press, and online, different target groups are being involved in developing the Estonian-language Wikipedia.[32]

Language Requirements and Language Support for Students

There are no unified admittance requirements for language skills in Estonia for Estonian or any foreign language. Institutions of higher education have also not set any language requirements to admit students to Estonian-medium curricula if the student has acquired the previous level of education in Estonian. The language of instruction in upper secondary school in Estonia is either Estonian only or 60 % Estonian in bilingual schools. A bilingual school gives its graduate a B2 level Estonian skill which is not quite sufficient for Estonian-medium university studies; a suitable level would be C1.

Institutions of higher education have developed specific requirements for graduates of bilingual schools and persons who have acquired the general education in another language. They need to provide proof of passing an Estonian language test (the state examination of Estonian as a second language, the test of B2 or higher level, the exam taken for graduation from IB DP or European School). The minimum score for the state exam or the B2 level test varies from 30 (EBS) to 80 points (UT). If the student cannot prove his or her Estonian skills the exam or test can be taken as part of the admission process.

Estonia provides free in-depth Estonian language studies for up to one year for those whose Estonian skills are insufficient to study in Estonian (CRI 2013). However, this opportunity is only used by approximately one-fifth of the students who come from bilingual or Russian-medium upper secondary schools.

Institutions of higher education have developed flexible ways to increase the students' Estonian skills without increasing the time of their studies by offering language courses on an appropriate level, support seminars, etc. The students' academic communication skills are also developed in writing and speech, as well as their knowledge of terminology, etc.

Conclusion

Significant changes have taken place in the sociolinguistic environment of independent Estonia in the last decades. Russian, which used to be the greatest influencing language for Estonian during the Soviet occupation, has been replaced by English—the main influencing language of the globalized world. Nevertheless, Estonian, which is the official language of Estonia and one of the official languages of the European Union, is still the primary language of higher education in Estonia. This ensures the flawless functioning of the Estonian language in Estonian education and research as well as all other spheres of social life in which experts with higher education degrees act. At the same time, the internationalisation of research and higher education is mainly mediated by English. Like many other countries, Estonia must seek a balance between the national and international component in higher education and occasionally duplicate publishing and other activities in different languages. The third language in Estonia, mainly of domestic importance, is Russian, whose role in higher education has been decreasing steadily since Russian-medium higher education does not ensure a level of official language skills necessary for the Estonian labour market. Whether English-medium curricula ensure the official language skills and knowledge of Estonia necessary for working in Estonia is another question. Many English-medium curricula lack the subjects of Estonian language and knowledge of Estonian society. Graduates of international curricula complain about their poor integration into Estonian society and leave Estonia even after receiving an education financed by the Estonian taxpayer.[33]

With regard to the levels of education, the tendency for the proportion of English to increase can be seen at the master's level, but especially in doctoral studies. Almost all doctoral programmes use English beside Estonian and the language of dissertations and defenses has been approximately 90 % English already for years. Although the internationalisation of research and higher education and the Estonian education reform have brought about the gradual increase in the role of English in higher education, Estonian continues to function as a language of research with the help of national measures: doctoral dissertations are also written in Estonian, dissertations written in a foreign language include resumes in Estonian (the sufficient length of the resumes is another matter), numerous textbooks for institutions of higher education are being compiled in Estonian, and 11 high-class academic journals are published in Estonian.

The visions and programmes of education currently in force pay less attention to preserving Estonian as a language of higher education. While just a decade ago one could confidently claim that Estonia's national regulations, development plans and programmes fully supported the use and development of Estonian in all spheres, including higher education and research, the higher education programme currently in force lacks clearly stated principles and measures to ensure the sustainability of Estonian as a language of higher education. Admittedly, we have support activities for developing textbooks and terminology, as well as for studying the Estonian language, but we lack the state-approved principle to preserve Estonian-medium higher education in the future. At the same time, as a positive shift on a political level, there were parliamentary debates in 2017 and 2018 on the preservation of the position of Estonian in higher education, numerous media activities related to the issue, the fact that the higher education language policy reached the party manifestos and the coalition contract in 2019. The necessity and the state's duty to ensure the sustainability of the Estonian language in all spheres of life, including higher education and research, is again gaining its place beside internationalisation as the developmental priority for the academic environment.

Universities develop curricula to compensate for the decrease in Estonian students by enrolling more foreign students and at the same time to adhere to national visions of internationalizing the institutions of higher education. This has led to a situation where English-medium curricula together with Estonian- and English-medium curricula constituted 30 % of all curricula in the academic year 2017–18.

At the moment, the increase in the number of English-medium curricula has lessened. In the course of the general decrease of the number of curricula in the academic year 2018–19, the proportion of the English-medium curricula remains at 25 % of all curricula. Nevertheless, at master's level 38 % of curricula are English-medium. And as was shown in the study on 'The State of Language in Estonia' (Lukk et al., 2017, p. 48): for the preservation of Estonian as a language of higher education, developing attitudes and sensing personal responsibility are even more important than national measures.

Notes

1. See online: http://www.efnil.org/, accessed on 4 Feb. 2018.
2. See online: https://www.youtube.com/watch?v=Y46uOG8kOT0&t=267s, accessed on 12 Apr. 2019.

3. See online: https://www.riigikogu.ee/pressiteated/taiskogu/riigikogus-oli-riikliku-tahtsusega-kusimusena-arutelu-eesti-keele-olukord/, accessed on 12 Apr. 2019.
4. We thank Ingrid Jaggo, Kalmer Lauk, Eero Loonurm and Tiia Margus for their help in acquiring the data.
5. See online: https://www.stat.ee/stat-rahvaarv-aasta-alguses.
6. See online: http://www.kul.ee/sites/kulminn/files/6_faktileht_a4_keelteoskus.pdf.
7. See online: https://www.kul.ee/sites/kulminn/files/le_rakendusplaani_aruanne_2017.pdf.
8. The data about the number of university students and curricula are based on the Estonian Educational Information System (EEIS). The data for the 2018–19 academic year reflect the situation as of 5 April 2019, cf. https://www.haridussilm.ee/.
9. See Chapter 1, section 1.
10. See Chapter 2, section 3(1).
11. See online: https://www.keeleinspektsioon.ee/en.
12. See Chapter 2, section 7.
13. See online: https://www.sirp.ee/s1-artiklid/varia/htmi-veerg-keelevaldkonnale-tahendusrikas-aasta-2019/.
14. See online on the webpage of the Ministry of Education and Research: https://www.hm.ee/et/tegevused/eesti-keel-ja-voorkeeled/programmid, accessed on 4 Feb. 2018.
15. See online: https://www.keeletehnoloogia.ee/en.
16. See online: https://www.hm.ee/sites/default/files/12_keeleprogramm_2018-2021.pdf.
17. See online: https://www.hm.ee/sites/default/files/lisa_eestikeeelsete_korgkooliopikute_loomise_toetamise_pohimotted_2018-2027_002.pdf.
18. See online: https://www.hm.ee/sites/default/files/eesti_keel_ja_kultuurimalu_ii_2014-2018.pdf.
19. See online: https://www.hm.ee/sites/default/files/strateegia2020.pdf, accessed on 15 Sep. 2017.
20. See online: https://www.hm.ee/sites/default/files/lisa_8_korghariduse_programm_2016-2019.pdf, accessed on 15 Sep. 2017.
21. See online: https://arvamus.postimees.ee/6520040/birute-klaas-lang-keelepoliitikast-valimisprogrammides.
22. See online: https://www.keskerakond.ee/files/Eesti-Keskerakonna-valimisplatvorm-Riigikogu-2019-valimistel.pdf.
23. See online: https://www.google.com/search?q=eesti+200+programm&oq=Eesti+200&aqs=chrome.1.0l6.4333j0j4&sourceid=chrome&ie=UTF-8.
24. See online: https://valimised2019.sotsid.ee/sotsiaaldemokraatide-programm-2019-aasta-riigikogu-valimisteks-igauks-loeb/.
25. See online: https://isamaa.ee/rk19programm/.
26. See online: https://www.riigikogu.ee/pressiteated/taiskogu/riigikogus-oli-riikliku-tahtsusega-kusimusena-arutelu-eesti-keele-olukord/.
27. See online: https://vabaerakond.ee/programm/.
28. See online: https://www.reform.ee/programm.
29. The totals also include the number of students with two languages of instruction which is not shown on a separate row in the table.

30. A total of all curricula, including the curricula of integrated bachelor's and master's studies, and of professional higher education not included in the table.
31. Since 1 September 2016, curricula in Estonia are classified according to the version ISCED-F 2013.
32. See online: http://www.miljonpluss.ut.ee/, accessed on 5 Feb. 2018.
33. Study of Estonian institutions of higher education graduates of 2015: https://www.hm.ee/sites/default/files/uuringud/vil2015_aruanne.pdf, accessed on 5 Feb. 2018.

References

AA 2012, *Ülikooliseaduse, rakenduskõrgkooli seaduse ja teiste seaduste muutmise seadus* [The Act Amending the Universities Act, the Institutions of Professional Higher Education Act and Other Acts] (2012), <https://www.riigiteataja.ee/akt/130052012001>, accessed on 4 Feb. 2018.

Canagarajah, Suresh, 'Lingua Franca English, Multilingual Communities, and Language Acquisition', *The Modern Language Journal* 91/1 (2007), 923–939.

Coalition Contract, *Eesti Reformierakonna, Sotsiaaldemokraatliku Erakonna ja erakonna Isamaa ja Res Publica Liit kokkulepe valitsuse moodustamise ja valitsusliidu tegevusprogrammi põhialuste kohta* [The Contract for Formation of the Goverment and the Foundations of the Coalition's Action Plan between the Estonian Reform Party, the Social Democratic Party and the Union of Isamaa and Res Publica], Eesti Reformierakond (2015), <https://www.reform.ee/koalitsioonilepe-2015-2016-re-sde-irl>.

Coalition Contract, *Eesti Keskerakonna, Sotsiaaldemokraatliku Erakonna ning Isamaa ja Res Publica Liidu valitsusliidu aluspõhimõtted 2016–2019* [The Foundations of the Coalition of the Estonian Centrist Party, the Social Democratic Party and the Union of Isamaa and Res Publica 2016–2019], Keskerakond (2016) < https://keskerakond.ee/files/valitsusliidu_aluspohimotted_2016-2019.pdf>.

Coalition Contract, *Eesti Keskerakonna, Eesti Konservatiivse Rahvaerakonna ning Isamaa Erakonna valitsusliidu aluspõhimõtted 2019–2023* [The Foundations of the Coalition of the Estonian Centrist Party, the Estonian Conservative People's Party and the Isamaa Party 2019–2023] (2019), <https://g1.nh.ee/images/pix/eesti-keskerakonna-eesti-konservatiivse-rahvaerakonna-ning-isamaa-erak-85835107.pdf>.

CRI, *Kõrghariduse omandamisel süvendatult riigikeele õppimise tingimused ja kord, Haridus- ja teadusminister* [Conditions and Regulations for in-depth Official Language Learning in the Course of Acquiring Higher Education] (Revision 2013), <https://www.riigiteataja.ee/akt/104012013022?leiaKehtiv>, accessed on 4 Feb. 2018.

Crystal, David, *Language death* (Cambridge: Cambridge University Press, 2002).

DPEL, 'Eesti keele arengukava 2011–2017' [Development Plan for the Estonian Language], Estonian Language Council (2011), <http://ekn.hm.ee/system/files/Eesti_keele_arengukava_2011-2017_0.pdf>, accessed on 4 Feb. 2018.

DSEL, 'Eesti keele arendamise strateegia 2004–2010' [Development Strategy of the Estonian Language], Estonian Language Council (2004), <http://ekn.hm.ee/system/files/strat_et.pdf>, accessed on 4 Feb. 2018.

DSELD, 'Keel loob väärtust. Eesti keelevaldkonna arengukava 2018–2027 (eelnõu)' [Language Creates Value. Development Strategy of the Estonian Language Domain 2018–2027 (draft)], Haridus- ja Teadusministeerium (2017).

ECR, Rektorite Nõukogu [Council of Rectors], <http://www.ern.ee/et>, accessed on 4 Feb. 2018.

EEIS, Eesti hariduse infosüsteem [Estonian Educational Information System], <http://www.ehis.ee/>, accessed on 4 Feb. 2018.

Ehala, Martin, 'Refining the Notion of Ethnolinguistic Vitality', *International Journal of Multilingualism* 7/4 (2010), 363–378.

Ehala, Martin, Kadri Koreinik, Kristiina Praakli, and Maarja Siiner, 'Kuidas uurida keele kestlikkust' [How to Study the Sustainability of Language], *Keel ja Kirjandus* 7 (2014), 489–507.

EHDR, Eesti Koostöö Kogu, *Eesti inimarengu aruanne 2007* [Estonian Human Development Report 2007] (Tallinn: Eesti Koostöö Kogu, 2008), <https://kogu.ee/public/trykised/EIA07_est.pdf>, accessed on 1 Jun. 2019.

EHEIS, *Eesti kõrghariduse rahvusvahelistumise strateegia* [The Estonian Higher Education Internationalisation Strategy], <https://www.hm.ee/sites/default/files/k6rghariduse_rahvusvahelistumise_strateegia.pdf>, accessed on 4 Feb. 2018.

EHES, *Eesti kõrgharidusstrateegia 2006–2015* [Estonian Higher Education Strategy 2006–2015], <https://www.riigiteataja.ee/akt/12752949>, accessed on 4 Feb. 2018.

ERIS, Eesti teadusinfosüsteem [Estonian Research Information System], <https://www.etis.ee/>, accessed on 4 Feb. 2018.

Estonian Constitution, *Eesti Vabariigi Põhiseadus* [Republic of Estonia Constitution] (2011), <https://www.riigiteataja.ee/akt/115052015002>, accessed on 4 Feb. 2018.

Fabricius, Anne, Janus Mortensen, and Hartmut Haberland,'The Lure of Internationalisation: Paradoxical Discourses of International Student Mobility, Linguistic Diversity and Cross-cultural Exchange', *Higher Education* 73/4 (2017), 577–595.

Haberland, Hartmut, and Janus Mortensen, 'Language Variety, Language Hierarchy and Language Choice in the International University', *International Journal of the Sociology of Language* 216 (2012), 1–6.

Hagege, Claude, *Combat pour le Français: Au nom de la diversité des langues et des cultures* (Paris: Odile Jacob, 2006).

Hakulinen, Auli, et al., *Suomen kielen tulevaisuus. Kielipoliittinen toimintaohjelma* (Kotimaisten kielten tutkimuskeskuksen verkkojulkaisuja 7, 2009), <https://www.hm.ee/sites/default/files/uuringud/oppekeel_eesti_korgkoolides_statistiline_ylevaade.pdf>, accessed on 17 May 2019.

IDPEL, 'Eesti keele arengukava 2011–2017 elluviimise vahearuanne (2011–2012)' [Interim Report on the Implementation of the 'Development Plan for the Estonian Language 2011–2017' (2011–2012)], Eesti keelenõukogu (2013), <http://ekn.hm.ee/node/57>, accessed on 27 Nov. 2014.

IDPEL, Eesti Keele Sihtasutus, *Eesti keele arengukava 2011–2017; elluviimise vahearuanne (2013–2014)* [Interim Report on the Implementation of the 'Development Plan for the Estonian Language 2011–2017' (2013–2014)] (Tallinn: 2015), <https://www.hm.ee/sites/default/files/eesti_keele_arengukava_2011-2017_elluviimise_vahearuanne_2013-2014.pdf>, accessed on 4 Feb. 2018.

IPHEA, *Rakenduskõrgkooli seadus 1998* [Institutions of Professional Higher Education Act], <https://www.riigiteataja.ee/akt/920764?leiaKehtiv>, accessed on 4 Feb. 2018.

Klaas, Birute, 'Eesti keele õpetamisest ja uurimisest võõrkeelena ja teise keelena Tartu ülikoolis' [On the Teaching and Study of Estonian as a Foreign Language and a Second Language at the University of Tartu], in Mati Erelt, ed., *200 aastat eesti keele ülikooliõpet* (Tartu: Tartu Ülikooli Kirjastus, 2003).

Klaas-Lang, Birute, 'Eesti keel kõrgkoolis' [Estonian Language in an Institution of Higher Education], *Keel ja Kirjandus* 3 (2012), 229–231.

Klaas-Lang, Birute, 'Eesti keele nähtavusest maailmas' [On the Visibility of the Estonian Language in the World], in Tiit Hennoste, ed., *Rahvusvahelised rahvusteadused* (Tartu: Tartu Ülikooli Kirjastus, 2014a), 131–146.

Klaas-Lang, Birute, 'L'état de la langue estonienne au début du 3XIe siècle', *Etudes finno-ougriennes* 44 (2014b), 31–58.

Klaas-Lang, Birute, 'State Policies and Institutional Language Choice—The Vitality of Estonian, Latvian and Lithuanian in Higher Education', in Marián Sloboda, Petteri Laihonen, and Anastassia Zabrodskaja, eds, *Sociolinguistic Transition in Former Soviet and Eastern Bloc Countries: Recent Developments Two Decades after the Regime Change* [Series of *Prague Papers on Language, Society and Interaction*] (Frankfurt am Main: Peter Lang, 2016), 235–262.

Klaas-Lang, Birute, 'Eesti keelevaldkonna arendamisest—vaade keelenõukogu seest' [On the Development of the Language Domain in Estonia—A View from within the Language Council], *Oma keel* 1 (2017), 66–72, <http://www.emakeeleselts.ee/omakeel/2017_1/OK-1-2017_11.pdf>.

Klaas-Lang, Birute, and Helle Metslang, 'Language Policy and Sustainability of Estonian in Higher Education', in Gerhard Stickel and Cecilia Robustelli, eds, *Language Use in University Teaching and Research. Contributions to the Annual Conference 2014 of EFNIL in Florence* [Series of Duisburg Papers on Research in Language and Culture 109] (Frankfurt am Main: Peter Lang, 2015), 161–177.

Klaas-Lang, Birute, and Helle Metslang, 'Eesti keele kestlikkus kõrghariduses' [On the Sustainability of Estonian in Higher Education], *Akadeemia* 4 (2018), 667–690.

Kuteeva, Maria, 'The Parallel Language Use of Swedish and English: The Question of "Nativeness" in University Policies and Practicea', *Journal of Multilingual and Multicultural Development* 35/4 (2014), 332–344.

Language Act, *Eesti NSV Keeleseadus 1989* [Estonian Soviet Socialist Republic Language Act], <http://estlex.com/tasuta/index.php?id=8&aktid=364&asutus=23&fd=1&grupp=1&leht=17>, accessed on 27 Nov. 2014.

Language Act, *Eesti Vabariigi keeleseadus 2011* [Republic of Estonia Language Act], <https://www.riigiteataja.ee/akt/118032011001?leiaKehtiv>, accessed on 4 Feb. 2018.

Lindström, Jan, 'Different Languages, One Mission? Outcomes of Language Policies in a Multilingual University Context', *International Journal of the Sociology of Language* 216 (2012), 33–54.

Lukk, Maarika, Kadri Koreinik, Kristjan Kaldur, Virve-Anneli Vihman, Anneli Villenthal, Kats Kivistik, Martin Jaigma, and Anastasia Pertšjonok, *Eesti keeleseisund* [The State of Language in Estonia] (Tartu: Tartu ülikool ja Balti Uuringute Instituut, 2017).

Mål i Mun—Förslag till handlingsprogram för svenska språket (Stockholm: Betänkande av Kommittén för svenska språket, SOU 2002:27).

Naidoo, Rajani, and Ian Jamieson, 'Knowledge in the Market Place: The Global Commodification of Teaching and Learning in Higher Education', in Peter Ninnes and Meeri Hellstén, eds, *International Higher Education: Critical Explorations of Pedagogy and Policy* (Dordrecht: Springer, 2005), 37–52.

ÕPLeht, 'Uus keele arengukava kütab kirgi' [The New Development Plan for Language Causes Emotions to Run High], Õpetajate Leht (2018), <http://opleht.ee/2018/02/uus-keele-arengukava-kutab-kirgi/>.

Phillipson, Robert, *English Only Europe? Challenging Language Policy* (London: Routledge, 2003).

Phillipson, Robert, *Linguistic Imperialism Continued* (London: Routledge, 2009).

Risager, Karen, 'Language Hierarchies at the International University', *International Journal of the Sociology of Language* 216 (2012), 111–130.

Rozenvalde. Kerttu, 'Multilayered Language Policy in Higher Education in Estonia and Latvia. Case of National Universities', doctoral dissertation, University of Latvia, Riga, <https://dspace.lu.lv/dspace/bitstream/handle/7/46471/298-68345-Rozenvalde_Kerttu_kk11232.pdf?sequence=1&isAllowed=y>.

Saarinen, Taina, 'Internationalization of Finnish Higher Education—Is Language an Issue?', *International Journal of the Sociology of Language* 216 (2012), 157–173.

Selliov, Rena, *Õppekeel Eesti kõrgkoolides EHISe andmetel. Statistiline ülevaade* [Language of Instruction in Estonian Institutions of Higher Education on the Basis of EEIS. Statistical Overview] (Tartu: Haridus- ja Teadusministeerium, 2017).

SHE, *Kõrgharidusstandard 2008* [Standard of Higher Education], <https://www.riigiteataja.ee/akt/13255227?leiaKehtiv>, accessed on 4 Feb. 2018.

Skutnabb-Kangas, Tove, *Linguistic Genocide in Education—Or Worldwide Diversity and Human Rights?* (Mahwah, NJ: Lawrence Erlbaum, 2000).

Soler-Carbonell, Josep, 'Els reptes de les llengües mitjanes a Catalunya i Estònia en l'era "glocal". Una perspectiva comparada de les ideologies lingüístiques dels seus parlants' [The Challenges of Medium-sized Languages in Catalonia and Estonia in the "Glocal" Era; A Comparative Perspective of their Speakers' Language Ideologies], *Revista de Llengua i Dret* 57 (2012), 207–248.

Soler-Carbonell, Josep, 'University Language Policies and Language Choice Among Ph.D Graduates in Estonia: The (Unbalanced) Interplay between English and Estonian', *Multilingua. Journal of Cross-Cultural and Interlanguage Communication* 33/3–4 (2014), 413–436.

Soler, Josep, *Language policy and the internationalization of universities* (Berlin/Boston: De Gruyter Mouton, 2019).

Soler, Josep, and Virve-Anneli Vihman, 'Language Ideology and Language Planning in Estonian Higher Education: Nationalising and Globalising Discourses', *Current Issues in Language Planning*, 19/1 (2018), 22–41.

Söderlundh, Hedda, 'Global Policies and Local Norms: Sociolinguistic Awareness and Language Choice at an International University', *International Journal of the Sociology of Language* 216 (2012), 87–109.

Stickel, Gerhard, and Cecilia Robustelli, eds, *Language Use in University Teaching and Research. Contributions to the Annual Conference 2014 of EFNIL in Florence* [Series of Duisburg Papers on Research in Language and Culture 109] (Frankfurt am Main, Peter Lang, 2015).

UA, *Ülikooliseadus 1995* [Universities Act], <https://www.riigiteataja.ee/akt/110072012028?leiaKehtiv>, accessed on 4 Feb. 2018.

UNESCO, 'ISCED: International Standard Classification of Education', UNESCO Institute for Statistics, <http://uis.unesco.org/en/topic/international-standard-classification-education-isced>, accessed on 4 Feb. 2018.

UNESCO, *ISCED Fields of Education and Training 2013 (ISCED-F 2013)* (Montreal: UNESCO Institute for Statistics, 2014), <https://eqe.ge/res/docs/228085e.pdf>, accessed on 17 May 2019.

Vertovec, Steven, 'Super-diversity and its Implications', *Ethnic and Racial Studies* 30/6 (2007), 1024–1054.

Vertovec, Steven, 'Towards Post-multiculturalism? Changing Communities, Contexts and Conditions of Diversity', *International Social Science Journal* 199 (2010), 83–95.

Vilà, Xavier F., and Vanessa Bretxa, eds, *Language Policy in Higher Education: The Case of Medium-Sized Languages* (Bristol: Multilingual Matters, 2014).

Frans Gregersen

The Nordic Response to Anglification of University Activities

The Nordic languages have a long history of mutual attraction and resistance. For this chapter they may conveniently be divided into the three central Scandinavian languages, i.e. Norwegian (incl. Bokmål and Nynorsk), Danish and Swedish (incl. Finland Swedish), and Icelandic and Finnish. Central questions for the Nordic language area are: how do language policies at the inter-Nordic level and within the nation state promote inter-Nordic communication through the use of one or more Scandinavian languages, and how do the five Nordic states face the challenge of English as the medium of international communication, not least at universities? This chapter deals with these central questions: it will outline how the inter-Nordic language cooperation has developed since the Second World War, and detail the language use at universities in the Nordic countries.

Keywords: language policy, parallel language use, Nordic countries, higher education, internationalisation

Introduction: Language Policy in the Nation State

Language policy is not an area endowed with ministries and much prestige, neither is it at the top of the political agenda and yet, language policy specialists would argue, it pervades everyday life in modern nation states (Wright 2016). The reason is that language policy includes all decisions taken within a community which have, or can be shown to have, linguistic consequences. This ranges from the choice of having street names in two languages in an officially bilingual city or nation state to the handwritten note in Arabic put up in a shop in a district in a city, e.g. Copenhagen, saying that the owner will be back soon. Obviously, there is much more politics in the strict sense of the word involved in the street name decision than in the handwritten note decision, but the fact that the language is used in the public domain in the latter case may be crucial for the development of a language policy in the strict sense. A language policy is accordingly *any statement regulating the use of linguistic resources in places where this may be regulated*. The point of departure for this contribution is that language policies are not only developed and put in place in the nation state but also in some cases at the regional level. This is the case for the Nordic region, which is the subject of this chapter. But before we enter the Nordic region we have to briefly outline the recent history of language policy making in the various nation states which make up this region.

Recent History of Language Policy Initiatives in the Nation States Belonging to the Nordic Region

In 1997 Ulf Teleman and Margareta Westman published a significant paper entitled 'Behöver Sverige en nationell språkpolitik?' ('Does Sweden need a national language policy?'). This became the starting point for a heated debate and later a parliamentary report entitled *Mål i mun* (which is difficult to translate but 'Speech in Mouth' might be the closest equivalent). A number of papers have commented on the Swedish process, the outcome and the consequences (Airey 2004; Hult 2003; Boyd and Huss 2004) but the important point here is that this Swedish initiative was copied all over the Nordic region in the next decade resulting in national language policies in Iceland and Finland and governmental initiatives in Norway and Denmark.

The main theme to be discussed was the place of the local Nordic language in the linguistic diversity created by on the one hand the recognition of old minority languages within the nation state (Sami and Eskimo are the obvious cases in point) and on the other hand the new immigrant languages which are spoken by sizeable minorities in the Nordic nation states, primarily in the main cities (see Quist and Svendsen 2010 for a review of the Scandinavian spoken by multilingual urban youngsters, and Kirchmeier-Andersen 2015 for the number of languages spoken (in Denmark only)).

The domains which lend themselves to language planning are the media, in so far as the Nordic welfare states have national media production systems (but the satellites are far beyond any national language planning efforts) which are supported by public money, the educational system and to a certain extent the cultural system of production of national language films and television series. Also tourism might have been brought into the picture, but as far as language use goes, this seems to have been left for the cultural and commercial stakeholders to manage.

A language which may be used in all of these domains and in the public debates, the legal system and the various administrative bodies may be called 'complete' and 'essential to society', a terminology first coined by the Swedish authors of the *Mål i mun* report but a terminology which has resonated in all subsequent initiatives, including the Nordic declaration of language policy to be described below (see section on 'The Nordic Declaration of Language Policy').

Regional Collaboration on Language Policy: The Nordic Case

The Nordic Region

Regions may be delimited from a number of perspectives: geographically, politically, historically, linguistically. In the case of the Nordic region all of these have to be used.

Geographically, the Nordic region includes the northernmost part of Europe (but does not include the other states around the Baltic although there is also some collaboration with the Baltic states, Estonia, Latvia and Lithuania, under the auspices of the Nordic region). Politically, the Nordic region includes five sovereign states: Iceland, Denmark, Norway, Sweden and Finland, but that means also the inclusion of the relatively independent regions of the Faroe Islands and Greenland (with Denmark as the state) and Åland (with Finland as the state). The delimitation of precisely these five states as making up a region rests on a historical and geographical basis and engenders some linguistic diversity within the region.

It is only to be explained by political history that Greenland and the Faroe Islands 'belong' to Denmark and are thus included. From a geographical point of view these communities would rather make up a North Atlantic region together with Iceland possibly (as is the case with Greenland) with strong ties across the Atlantic to regions of Canada and the United States where other Eskimo-speaking people are located. Linguistically, Eskimo is not understandable or related to the Northwest Germanic branch of Germanic, which Faroese and Icelandic belong to.

The relationship between Finland and Sweden is also a historico-political fact with a strong Swedish presence in Finlandic institutions and education and some Finnish presence in a part of Sweden, notably Tornedalen. However, after the Napoleonic wars, Russia annexed Finland, and Sweden included Norway, which until then had been part of the Danish kingdom for centuries. Finland is by law a bilingual nation with constitutional protection of the Swedish language in a number of respects, some of which are highly relevant in what follows. For an interesting recent comparison of Finland and the Baltic states of Estonia and Latvia see Soler (2019).

Norway, Sweden and Finland as sovereign states include a large number of Sami-speaking people. The division of the various Sami languages or dialects is a subject not to be mentioned further here (see http://samer.se/sprak), but it bears mention that recent estimated figures of individuals of Sami descent are 50–65,000 in Norway, 20–40,000 in Sweden, and only around 8,000 in Finland (http://samer.se/samernaisiffror).

Finally, there are large minorities of immigrants in the Nordic countries. From a linguistic point of view it is notable how little we know about their home languages (Ag 2018 is an interesting discussion of this in the Danish context). It has been estimated that around 200 languages are present in Denmark but some of them have very few speakers and only the Turkish, Urdu, Farsi, Somali and Arabic minorities are large enough to make themselves visible to the public eye.

Summing up, the national languages of the Nordic region are for a large part historically related, though not necessarily mutually understandable anymore: Icelandic and Faroese differ in structure from Norwegian, Swedish and Danish, although all of them are North Germanic languages. Eskimo, however, is a branch of its own, and Finnish and Sami are Fenno-Ugrian languages. The mutual intelligibility of Nordic citizens thus rest on the precondition that pupils in school are presented with specimina of each others' languages and the idea that all Icelanders are bilingual with Danish as their second language and that all Finnish people also learn Swedish sufficiently to both speak it and understand it. In that case, Swedish may be the obvious *lingua franca* but at most inter-Nordic events most people speak their own language and strive to understand that of others. It does, in fact, sometimes happen that this works—to the surprise of innocent foreign bystanders or eavesdroppers!

A recent case has shown that the pessimism expressed in the most recent empirical investigation of the receptive competence of Nordic pupils (Delsing and Lundin Åkesson 2005) may be overstated or simply not possible to uphold. The Norwegian television series SKAM was a pathbreaking series for Norwegian youngsters which reached hitherto unthinkable numbers of viewers in the target population. But the fact was that Danish youngsters started viewing this series (possibly with the vital support of the text messages which abound in the series) before it was screened by the Danish Radio (Bergløv 2016). This example has been taken to show that when the right elements are there, youngsters in a country which was thought to be linguistically quite far removed from the two other Scandinavian countries are in fact able to understand a programme even though it is in another Scandinavian language (Quist and Skovse 2017).

Nordic Collaboration, the Framework

The Nordic states have collaborated since the Helsinki Treaty of 1962 laid down the foundations of their cooperation. The most relevant paragraph for this paper is article 8(2) on cultural cooperation:[1]

> Educational provision in the schools of each of the Nordic countries shall include an appropriate measure of instruction in the languages, cultures and general social

> conditions of the other Nordic countries, including the Faeroe Islands, Greenland and the Åland Islands. (Helsinki Treaty 2018)

Three observations: firstly, not only the member states but also the home ruled countries such as the Faroe and Åland Islands and Greenland are included. Secondly, probably for that very reason there is an important rider: "*an appropriate measure* of instruction" (emphasis added). And thirdly: this is placed under the heading of 'cultural collaboration', not educational, although it obviously would have been more effective to state the aim in educational terms. This is significant since nothing in principle would have prevented the five states from agreeing that their educational systems should include introductions to the neighbouring languages in some measure, preferably enough to secure mutual understanding of the spoken Scandinavian languages.

This, however, is not the case with the Helsinki Treaty and in my view the Nordic collaboration has since then been trying to remedy this deplorable state of affairs. It has not succeeded and probably never will if the current approach of supplementing otherwise entirely national systems with a Nordic twist prevails.

The Nordic states set up a dual system of collaboration: the governments and civil servants collaborate under the heading of the Nordic Council of Ministers with a secretariat placed in Copenhagen while the five parliaments regularly meet under the auspices of the Nordic Council (see www.norden.org). There are elaborate systems of inter-Nordic committees to prepare matters for both councils and some funds which, however, have been severely reduced during the most recent decades.

Collaboration Until the New Wave of Language Policies (2003 ff)

According to Agazzi et al. (2014), characteristically entitled *Guldtavlorna i gräset*, the first fifty years of Nordic collaboration, i.e. after the Second World War, were a golden age where Nordic collaboration was firmly established with the various national language boards (*Sprognævn/Språknämnd/Språkråd*) as its recognized driving force. The boards singled out specific areas for collaboration such as *terminology*: it was deemed essential to alleviate Nordic collaboration by creating equivalent terms within the specific areas of traffic (e.g. SAS, which after all is an inter-Scandinavian airline), postal services and the media; in the field of *orthography* it was generally felt to be too late for breakthroughs (cf. Karker 1976), whereas genuine efforts were made to coordinate the creation of new general words to substitute for loanwords in the various Nordic *lexicons*.

In 1978 the Nordic Council of Ministers created a language secretariat to be the inter-Nordic institution which in close collaboration with the language boards would drive the efforts forward. The secretariat was, however, closed down in 1996 as part of a general purge of inter-Nordic institutions. It was felt that they were too costly and too inflexible to carry out the job in a changing environment. It was substituted by several advising committees which gradually became more or less independent of the language boards and drew their membership more from the universities.

The Nordic Declaration of Language Policy

In 2004–06 a declaration of a Nordic language policy was written and through a long process of inclusion of various interested parties finally accepted and endorsed by the Nordic Council of Ministers at a meeting in 2006 (the text may be found at <http://norden.diva-portal.org/smash/get/diva2:700895/FULLTEXT01.pdf>; this link will give you access to equivalent texts in all the Nordic languages but the link also includes an authorized English version). The background was the need felt at the Nordic Council of Ministers for a document that would be able to guide the efforts in the next period. Whether this goal has been reached or not is a matter for discussion. As I am writing this text, a process of revision has just been started at the Nordic Council of Ministers (Aurstad, pers. comm.).

The declaration consists of a preamble setting out the ministers' (and through them the five governments') intention of working in the direction set out in the document but states unequivocally that the document is not legally binding. Thus the various member states may wish to follow through on the declaration in different ways. Next follows an introduction which lays out the terminology used throughout:

> We in the Nordic countries consider all languages to be equal. They do not, however, all play the same role. A language may be *complete and essential to society* in relation to the language community in which it is spoken. A language is *complete* in this respect if it can be used in all areas of society. A language is *essential to society* if it is used in a language community for official purposes, for example education and legislation. There are six languages in the Nordic countries that are both complete and essential to society: Danish, Finnish, Faroese, Icelandic, Norwegian (in both written forms: Bokmål and Nynorsk), and Swedish. There is no one-to-one correlation between language and country, as shown e.g. by Finland, where both Finnish and Swedish are official national languages. There are two other languages that can be considered essential to society but cannot be used in all areas of society: the different varieties of Sami and Greenlandic. (Nordisk Ministerråd 2006, p. 91 (emphasis in original))

The distinction between languages which are complete and essential to society and those which are either not complete or not essential to society, leads to two interesting consequences: the first type is in need of support from the Nordic community (in order to become (more) complete). The second type may be termed mother tongues of Nordic residents which are not essential to society; these would be the minority languages and they should be supported by the Nordic member states (cf. below).

The declaration itself consists of two parts: the first one is concerned with the linguistic rights of Nordic residents (meaning all individuals who reside permanently in a Nordic country) and the aims of a Nordic language policy. The second part includes a description of the four issues to be worked with in the next period.

The first part on rights specifies these as follows:

> Nordic language policy is based on all Nordic residents having the right:
>
> - to acquire both spoken and written skills in a language essential to society, so that they can participate in the workings of society;
> - to acquire an understanding of and skills in a Scandinavian language and an understanding of the other Scandinavian languages so that they can take part in the Nordic language community;
> - to acquire a language of international importance so that they can take part in the development of world society;
> - to preserve and develop their mother tongue and their national minority language. (Nordisk Ministerråd 2006, p. 92)

A distinctive feature of this view of language is that it is a resource which makes it possible to take part in the communities which use this language for political purposes (voting and the debates leading up to elections). Thus this view of language prioritizes the citizen.

In accordance with this the declaration states the aims of a language policy as:

> - that all Nordic residents being able to read and write the language or languages that are essential to society in the area where they live;
> - that all Nordic residents being able to communicate with one another, preferably in a Scandinavian language;
> - that all Nordic residents having a basic knowledge of linguistic rights in the Nordic countries and the language situation in the Nordic countries;
> - that all Nordic residents having very good skills in at least one language of international importance and good skills in another foreign language;
> - that all Nordic residents having a general knowledge of what language is and how it works. (Nordisk Ministerråd 2006, p. 92–3)

The original declaration did not contain the final aim (which arguably is less essential for the citizen as such) but had an aim which was abolished in the process, i.e. that all Nordic residents get support for the development of their first language (L1). This was at a time when the Danish Government was concerned to reduce the national or community obligations to support immigrant language education in any other language than Danish.

The declaration's second part is concerned with the issues to work on and specifies them as follows:

- Language comprehension and language skills
- Parallel use of languages
- Multilingualism
- The Nordic region as a forerunner in Europe

The first issue is the central challenge of preparing the Nordic residents for common language practices. As outlined above the only possibility is to use one or more of the Scandinavian languages, Norwegian, Swedish or Danish. Icelanders have to settle for Danish (taught in schools), Norwegian (closer to the Icelandic language), or Swedish (the largest and most central language). Finnish citizens have to have Swedish as their L2 (or L1). In general, it is considered to be too ambitious to teach everyone in Scandinavia to speak the two neighbouring Scandinavian languages. Instead, the idea would be to teach perceptual skills such that any Nordic resident would be able to understand more or less distinctly pronounced and more or less slowly produced Scandinavian neighbouring languages. In practice the ambitions differ extremely, both in theory (when you look at the regulatory texts for the mother tongue across the various stages of the educational system) between the states, and in practice: no one can tell what actually happens in this field in the various nation states.

The third issue is focused on the challenge of the multilingual communities which have been created as fugitives and immigrants from various parts of the world have flocked to the cities of Europe whereas the fourth, somewhat self-congratulatory issue in practice is concerned with communication between public authorities and citizens, the so-called 'clear language initiatives' (*klarspråksinitiativ*).

The second issue (parallel use of languages) is of particular interest in this connection and will be treated in depth below based on the work of two successive inter-Nordic groups of researchers and administrators. But before I do that, I want to summarize the findings of the research in mutual language understanding in the Nordic region as a backdrop. After all, why treat the Nordic region as a region if it does not also make up some sort of linguistic community where at least some people understand the language of the other?

A Critical Appraisal of Selected Issues in Research on Mutual Language Understanding in the Nordic Region

Two Questionnaire Surveys: Haugen 1953 Compared to Kirchmeier and Skafte Jensen 2016

In 1953, the famous Norwegian-American linguist Einar Haugen (1906–1994), arguably the father of language planning as an academic discipline, published a questionnaire survey of inter-Nordic understanding. The survey was a pioneering effort inspired by the sociologist's use of this new technique ('The author is not a sociologist but a linguist and this is probably the first time a questionnaire has been used in this way to collect linguistic information' (Haugen 1953, p. 226)[2]). The study was republished in English in 1966 with the unfortunate title 'Semicommunication: The Language Gap in Scandinavia'. Semicommunication stuck as a term for imperfect understanding in Scandinavia.

The study is original in many respects: it is empirical (although as all questionnaire studies based on self-assessment); it is not only quantitative (apparently there were many open questions or invitations of comments included); it is sociologically sensitive, i.e. it only includes sociologically characterized informants; it is thorough, i.e. it covers both written and spoken modes, and introduces the study of language attitudes (but only focuses on perception, not production); and, finally, it is thoughtful, i.e. it does not just report its findings but seeks to explain them.

The sample includes 54 Swedes, 117 people from Norway and 81 from Denmark; a total of 252 persons (88 % males (!), partly because telephone listings were used and these were often in the male's name at that time). The sample is skewed towards the middle class and in particular academics. This has some interesting consequences.

The results may be summarized as follows: Sweden was at that time the most numerous, the wealthiest and the most prestigious country in the region, and this status of the nation state resulted in Swedish being the central language in the study, especially for Danes (Haugen 1953, p. 235, 248). The centrality shows in the figures for acquaintance where Haugen shows that Danes (and to a certain extent Norwegians) read Swedish literature but that the converse does not easily happen (Haugen 1953, p. 241). The real difference between the languages, however, was that Danish was seen as a language which not only was hard to understand but also valued less highly by its speakers and the neighbours alike than Swedish and Norwegian. As to class, Haugen succinctly concludes that Nordic collaboration is a matter for academics and that neither blue collar workers nor rural informants participate in a supra-national Nordic community.

In a review of Haugen 1976, Stig Örjan Ohlsson mentions a Sifo-Gallup questionnaire survey from 1973 commissioned by the Nordic Council which turned up some interesting new developments: the level of mutual understanding was assessed as having risen substantially (since Haugen's original study): almost complete understanding between Norwegians and Swedes (only spoken language!) and a level of 79 % to 85 % for Norwegians and Danes were reported. The only exception to the generalisation that mutual understanding had increased was the Swedes' understanding of spoken Danish; that had not changed at all and was still at 47 % (Ohlsson 1978a, p. 30).

Haugen's results may aptly be compared with the results which Sabine Kirchmeier and Eva Skafte Jensen got when they sent out a new questionnaire more than 60 years later (Kirchmeier and Jensen 2016). 648 informants from Scandinavia responded. The sample is comparable to Haugen's in that it is skewed towards people being active in Nordic work while there is a difference in the gender skewedness since the Kirchmeier-Jensen sample is mainly female (63 %). With 60 years apart these two studies seem comparable as to methods and sampling. So, which are the differences?

Haugen mentions that a strategy to overcome problems of mutual understanding might be to have recourse to a second common (foreign) language but interestingly he mentions all three main languages taught at the time, German, French and finally (and more rarely used) English. In the Kirchmeier and Jensen study only English may be used as a *lingua franca* and this of course represents the most essential change in the linguistic landscape. This is all the more significant in that the answers to language understanding point towards English being better understood (as evaluated by the informants themselves) than any of the Nordic languages: 85 % state that they have no problems with spoken English and the same figure is reported for written English. The comparable figures for Danish are only 41 % for speech, but 66 % for written Danish. Still, Swedish has a different position than either Danish or Norwegian in that the figure for understanding spoken Swedish is 53 %. For the written Scandinavian languages we may really talk about widespread perceived mutual understanding since in the neighbouring countries between 63 % (Norwegian) and 68 % (Swedish) report having no problems in understanding.

Experimental Studies: The Delsing and Lundin Åkesson 2005 Study

Until now, we have looked at questionnaire studies. In such studies informants are asked to evaluate their own competence and/or performance. Not so in the experimental studies we shall discuss below. Here all informants are set a task and are scored as to how well they perform on the task. To the best of my knowledge no one has yet combined the two in a design where informants were first asked to state their competence and then subjected to a test.

Nordic authorities had financed the first empirical study carried out as a rigorously designed controlled experiment in 1976, i.e. Maurud's classic study using (only male) recruits for military service as its sample and focusing on the capitals of Oslo, Stockholm and Copenhagen. The sample's obvious gender weakness and the focus on the capitals were pointed out quite early by Stig Örjan Ohlsson in three related papers (Ohlsson 1976, cf. Ohlsson 1978a, 1978b). In 2002 the Nordic foundation for cultural collaboration (Nordisk Kulturfond) took the decision to start a project which would be an updated and considerably enlarged version of Maurud's original study and hired Lars Olof Delsing to be the project's leader. The report, which is a cornerstone in the research tradition, appeared in 2005 and has the following characteristics:

- The scope is widened to encompass all potential informants from all Nordic languages but what is tested is their understanding of spoken and written Scandinavian Norwegian, Danish and Swedish—and English.
- The methods are much more sophisticated than Maurud's and include use of e.g. video clips as stimulus material, a method which seems well suited to the task of elucidating everyday understanding of the neighbouring languages.
- The sample is composed of high school students (and to a certain extent their parents) and consists of both L1 speakers and L2 speakers (this is a significant innovation).
- Finally, geographically both the contact zones between two neighbouring countries (e.g. Scania-Zealand) and the capitals (which are sometimes far removed from contact zones, e.g. Stockholm) are represented in the sample.

The results of the Delsing and Lundin Åkesson 2005 study may be summarized as follows:

- Compared with Maurud's results, inter-Scandinavian comprehension in the Delsing and Lundin Åkesson study seems to have decreased considerably (see their section 6.3, p. 120 ff).
- There is still a slight asymmetry between Danes and Swedes, but the general result is that among the central Scandinavians, the Norwegians are the masters of inter-Scandinavian comprehension (even though they were surpassed by the Faroese in all tests).
- Danish is far better understood in its written form than in its spoken form.

- English is in general better understood than any one of the Scandinavian languages.
- L2 speakers do not in general understand the neighbouring Scandinavian languages.

The results of the Delsing and Lundin Åkesson study were received with a global depression. Particularly the comparison between Maurud's results and the new results spread the news that inter-Scandinavian comprehension had decreased dramatically. This was bolstered by the comparison of the older group and the high school students, which manifested the same decrease. In sum, the results were interpreted as the end of Nordic inter-comprehension and the imminent danger of English as the *lingua franca* for youths was recalled as a most likely scenario. In the next section, I will document how a new series of studies have attempted to reverse this interpretation, but some critical remarks and reservations, mainly based on the frank discussion at the end of the study itself, may already be voiced here.

First, high school students are perhaps the least likely group to be interested in understanding neighbouring languages. Thus the choice of this group as representative for the population may be a mistake. From a pragmatic point of view, the value of the neighbouring languages is close to nil unless you fall in love with a person from one of the neighbouring communities. This might change when individuals leave the educational system and find a work place. We need to study e.g. the pragmatic situations which have arisen after the construction of the bridge between Sweden and Denmark, which allows many Swedes to work in Denmark. How do they manage? Which strategies do they use? Conversely a number of Danish firms work in Sweden in consulting, construction and in the pharmaceutical industry. How do they manage?

Secondly, the stimulus materials may have been under less control than originally thought. The authors point that out themselves when they discuss the relative ease of the various stimulus materials (Delsing and Lundin Åkesson 2005, p. 137).

Thirdly, the authors discuss a very interesting phenomenon which has to do with what we might call 'the capital syndrome'. Copenhageners perform badly in general on all the tests and Stockholmians are worse at understanding Danish than the Swedish-speaking Finns. Maybe the high school students in the capitals are the least interested in the neighbouring societies; they simply have their attention on other capitals instead. This is a very interesting discussion precisely because so much research has concentrated on the capitals, starting with Maurud's study.

The Positive Turn (Eva Theilgaard Brink 2016, Sonja Barfod Lund 2019)

Two recent Danish studies have used new methods. Eva Theilgaard Brink used interviews (the (qualitative) interview method was pioneered by Ulla Börestam in her 2008 portraits of multiple language users) to study migrants between the Nordic countries with a view to analysing how they themselves experienced their linguistic integration in the new country. The results are aptly summarized in the title 'You only have to throw yourself into it' (*Man skal bare kaste sig ud i det!*) and seem to clearly document a process from complete disorientation and lack of understanding through various attempts at repair, among them the use of English as a supplement, and finally to more or less complete functioning—and all that in the course of typically two to three months (for Finnish informants and Icelanders more likely five months).

Sonja Barfod Lund in her doctoral dissertation used an ethnographic approach to study multilingual interaction in business enterprises. In one of the firms she studied the use of the Nordic languages and this gave the impetus to a critical assessment of the study of inter-Nordic comprehension from Haugen up until today. This part of the original dissertation has been published separately as Barfod Lund 2019. Barfod Lund has the idea that the interpretation of results seems to vary although the results themselves do not; it simply depends on whether the researcher in question expects the informants to understand each other perfectly (in which case he or she is disappointed) or not (in which case he or she may be positively surprised). This is a valid critique and Barfod Lund has pointed to the fact that in actual interactive communication very few Scandinavians have said that they do not understand each other. In other words, there seems to be an inter-Nordic readiness to understand, an inter-Nordic potential. This is a very good basis for speakers working together to create a multilingual space of understanding, each person speaking his or her own language and understanding that of the others (cf. also the SKAM experience mentioned above).

The upshot of all this is that there are good reasons to view the Nordic region as a region where speakers have the potential to understand each other, not without any investment of attention and effort but still, with the result that they may understand each other. The most notable exception seems to be immigrant L2 speakers of a Nordic language. No one has as yet questioned the important result from the Delsing and Lundin Åkesson 2005 study that these Nordic residents do not seem to have the same potential for understanding the neighbouring Nordic languages as the L1 speakers (on the other hand, we have not yet seen a study which controls for L2 mastery). This has important consequences for a language policy which aims at integrating L2 speakers via university education and for the aim of the Nordic declaration of language policy that all citizens should be able to participate in the Nordic community.

Language Use at Universities in the Nordic Countries

Status as of 2014

In 2014 the organisation for the language boards in Europe, EFNIL, held a conference in Florence on 'Language Use in University Teaching and Research'. The papers from the conference were edited by Gerhard Stickel and Cecilia Robustelli and may be a handy way of introducing the status of 2014 as to language policies for higher education. Sabine Kirchmeier, who was then the director of the Danish Language Board and was called Kirchmeier-Andersen, gave an overview of the Danish system of universities and their various language policies with a concise description of ministerial initiatives and the various papers produced by the Language Board. Gudrun Kvaran covered Iceland in the same way, while Jan-Ola Östman gave a paper outlining the state of the Nordic region with special reference to Finland which I will come back to below (cf. Kirchmeier-Andersen 2015; Kvaran 2015; Östman 2015).

The presentations are all based on scattered, and to a certain extent incomparable, data. Everybody would agree that what we need data about are the following areas:

- Language policies—national as well as local, and if accepted, how are they put into practice?
- Scientific publications—how much is published in the local Nordic language and how much is published in English (or other foreign languages, but this rider seems to be academic in the most frequent sense of this word)?
- Mobility of students and staff
- Educational programmes—how many programmes are taught in English (i.e. with EMI as the international abbreviation for English-Medium Instruction)?

On all these subjects, the inter-Nordic group on parallel language policies at universities made an effort to dig up the most reliable data to be had. I will now outline the work of this group.

The Work of the Inter-Nordic Group on Parallel Language Policies: First Phase, the Descriptive Stance

Jan-Ola Östman, in his contribution to the EFNIL symposium in Florence 2014, gave an overview of the first phase of work of the Nordic Council of Ministers' group on parallel language policy. I refer to this description (Östman 2015) but detail selected issues below. To start out with an example: Table 5.1 details the available data on the pattern of scientific publications in the five Nordic states.

All numbers concern the percentage of the total of scientific publications which were published in the local Nordic language (for Finland both Finnish and Swedish). The Danish and Norwegian figures are for the whole country and concern the year 2010, while the figures for Sweden only concern selected disciplines as noted. Finally, the figures for Iceland are for doctoral theses only and concern only the University of Iceland, whereas the Finnish figures are for the University of Helsinki only.

As you can easily see, the table is extremely illustrative of the difference in publication language among the faculties (Health and Science do not publish much in the local language while the Social Sciences and Humanities publish between two thirds (Law in Sweden) of their papers and books and around a third (Social Science in Denmark) in the relevant Nordic language). But what is even more significant is that the data are strictly speaking incomparable.

Thus, the first major effort of the Nordic group on parallel language policies became to produce updated knowledge about the four areas detailed in the bullet list above for each country. The collected country reports were published in 2014 as *Hvor parallel* ('How parallel') with introductions on EMI and its consequences and on parallel language policies in general in 2014.

Since one of the lessons of this exercise was that it was possible to paint relatively comprehensive pictures for each country separately but that it was completely impossible to compare the pictures outlined since they were based on different (types of) data, the group concluded that it would be necessary for the Nordic Council of Ministers to get a more complete picture of the area by regulating the data collection so as to get the same data delimited in the same way for all Nordic member states. The result was the indicator report, which was published in 2017. I have chosen to refer to the English translation from the final report *More Parallel, Please* (about which more below) since I think it is a valid

Table 5.1: Publication in the Local Nordic Language within the Five Nordic Member States

FAC/COUNTRY	DK	IS	SE	NO	FI
Health	10	18	-	18	-
Science/ Tech.	3	3	0.5 (Physics)	5	4
Social Sciences	36	48	64 (Law)	50	50
Humanities	44	55	55 (Hist.)–15 (Ling.)	50	47

attempt to give the necessary definitions of what we are, or rather should be, counting when we speak of the reality behind language policies.

The indicators chosen are:

- As to language policy:
  - whether language policies have been drawn up for the individual institutions in the country concerned;
  - whether there are overarching guidelines at the national level, in the form of language legislation, white papers or similar.
- As to publications:
  - the total number of journal articles produced per annum in the country's university sector by main language and affiliation to main discipline or subject;
  - the number of PhD dissertations per annum by main language, taking into account the main discipline, the university at which it was defended and the date the dissertation was approved.
- As to the Nordic languages and English as teaching languages:
  - the total number of teaching hours advertised in a Nordic language vs. in English, in the university sector in the relevant year by main disciplines;
  - the total number of study programmes advertised in English in the relevant year, broken down by level (i.e. Bachelor compared to Master's) and main disciplines.
- As to mobility and internationalisation:
  - the total number of exchange students and full-degree students in the university sector in the relevant year, by level (i.e. Bachelor compared to Master's) and main disciplines;
  - the number of new international appointments per annum, defined as appointments of individuals who were not citizens of the country concerned prior to their appointment, and who were not resident in the country immediately prior to their appointment. (Gregersen et al., 2018, Appendix 65 f)

A few comments on the indicators:

The indicators are divided between the first ones on language policies which probably do not change that often, and the rest which are specified for every second year, since it is important to be able to pinpoint the trends through time. Apparently, the use of English in the domain of universities is spreading so quickly, albeit with interesting differences between disciplines and countries, that it does become possible indeed to spot trends rather fast, i.e. on the basis of e.g. a period of five years, once we have full control of the basic data.

Publication measures are most often documented in the various bibliometric systems. In Norway and Denmark these systems are national and so the figures are available in considerable detail. In Sweden some universities, e.g. Gothenburg, use the Norwegian system as well and in Iceland there are figures for the largely dominant university Háskóli Íslands in Reykjavik. We have chosen to focus on

PhD theses since they seem to be a reliable measure of the compromise between what young scholars want and what their supervisors advise them to do in terms of language and consequently may be used as a realistic proxy for future trends[3].

In the case of study programmes we were well aware of the fact that ethnographic research (Ljosland 2014; Söderlundh 2012) has pointed out that not all courses advertised in English are in fact EMI courses. On the other hand, it would be completely impossible to collect figures based on ethnographic research of this kind every other year. There seems to be a general trend in the Nordic countries to restrict the use of EMI to the master's level and PhD courses, but there are exceptions to this rule.

The Work of the Inter-Nordic Group on Parallel Language Policies: From the Descriptive Stance to the Normative One: Best Practices

It was inherent in the brief of the Nordic group on parallel language use at universities that it would end up giving advice on best practices. As described above, we based our work on a solid and relatively intensive first phase, detailing a description of how the facts were on the ground, based on the most valid available data. The data turned out not to be quite comparable but they were sufficient to make us aware of common tendencies and local exceptions. In the second phase of the work, we deliberately took another stance, the normative one. If we were to give advice on what a 'best practice' would look like, we would have to sharpen our ideas about what was good about good practices. We had long discussions on whether we would adopt a view of effective teaching and look at the numbers of students who failed or passed their exams or perform interviews with selected student bodies. We soon discarded this as too demanding in terms of comparative empirical studies and opted instead for studying the best practices at the universities in the Nordic region. Thus we arranged visits to universities in Copenhagen, Helsinki, Bergen, the Stockholm-Uppsala region and Reykjavik. A group also visited Nuuk, Greenland in order to learn about the problems of a university in a country with a less than complete language (cf. above section on 'Regional Collaboration'). Finally, another group visited Amsterdam, Maastricht and Luxemburg in order to learn from countries which in many ways resemble the Nordic region but still have a number of obvious differences, not least that of scale. Everywhere we met with the university administration and/or leadership and the local language policy expertise.[4]

On the basis of resumes of the visits carried out during this phase of the work we agreed on the following 11 recommendations:

1. Every university should have a language policy.
2. Every university should have a language policy committee.
3. Every university should have a language centre.
4. Staff recruited abroad should be offered courses in the teaching language, common speech and language for special purposes.
5. Various categories of students should be offered language courses, following needs analyses.
6. Lecturers and researchers should be offered language courses, following needs analyses.
7. Universities should choose their teaching languages based on the principles of parallel language use and the 'international classroom'.
8. University language policies should also cover the language used in the administration.
9. The universities should monitor and regularly reassess the choice of language for publications.
10. University language policies should also cover the language used in dissemination of knowledge, outreach and external communication activities.
11. Language policies should include developing digital language-support resources at every university. (Gregersen et al., 2018, p. 7)

The normative basis for these recommendations is the following: we believe that language policy is important for the simple reason that the choice of the language of instruction and other language policy decisions have—partly unknown—effects on the everyday functioning of universities. First of all, they have consequences for the quality of teaching: if teachers are not qualified to teach in another language than the local Nordic one, learning outcomes will suffer and teachers will get justifiably frustrated. Secondly, the choice of English instead of a Nordic language must have a reason and that reason has to be evident for those involved: teachers, admin, students, researchers, etc. Now, it follows that it will be wise to make all this explicit in a document which is available for all to read (and discuss—and revise …). And it follows from this that we need someone qualified to formulate the policy (a committee) and someone qualified (a centre) to put it into practice by educating and/or supporting teachers, students, researchers and admin. Obviously, universities work by harnessing knowledge and condensing it into practices. Language policy as a field of knowledge should not be any different and for that reason we recommended that the language centres were staffed with researchers as well as teachers. The area is dynamic and might change so quickly because of new knowledge that universities may fall by the wayside without even knowing it if they do not hire people who are active at the research front or at least are in touch with the domain. The rest of the recommendations seem to be about which areas a language policy should cover, but that is only in this first and simple version of the recommendations.

The recommendations are construed as an accordion. The first version of the recommendations is the one given above and in the summary. The next version adds a text arguing why this has been recommended and how it may be realized while the third version adds even more text based on our studies in the Nordic region and the Netherlands and detail the why and how even more. In this way, we make the text available to people who do not have the time to delve into details but still want to be informed as well as those who want to know why we have chosen this formulation and what it means.

Conclusion

I have argued that the Nordic region, for geographical and historical reasons, has created the possibility for its residents to navigate at least three Scandinavian languages (and for some of them this is in addition to their own L1). In this way a potential for a regional area of communication has been created. But the Nordic welfare states all face the challenge of internationalisation, which has meant that more and more courses are taught in English and more and more students and staff are attracted by this fact and thus fuel the process of anglification even more (Hultgren, Gregersen and Thøgersen 2014).

Nordic communication does not seem to be threatened by being replaced by an English *lingua franca* when it comes to everyday practices across borders (cf. the section on 'The Positive Turn' above). But in view of the facts which seem to persist throughout, i.e. that academics have been the torch bearers of the Nordic thought, it is possible that in the immediate present we might witness a trend towards using English as a common *lingua franca* at universities not only for local internationalisation but also for inter-Nordic internationalisation.

However, a counter trend has recently emerged and as I am writing this chapter, the yellow vests in France and the nationalistic currents in Eastern (Hungary) and Central Europe (Austria) as well as the Netherlands make it possible that we are presently entering a new phase where nationalistic resistance will also spread to universities and create a possible reversal to make only the 'complete and essential languages' of the Nordic region the recognized media of instruction once again.

Notes

1. There is a footnote stating that this paragraph has been given a new wording in 1983.
2. Original: 'Forfatteren er ikke sosiolog men språkforsker, og det er sannsynligvis förste gang et spörreskema blir brukt på denne måte for å samle språklige opplysninger'.
3. For the institutions, there is an economic benefit to be had from theses based on a number of articles published in (mostly) international journals since these in the bibliometric surveys are counted as such as well as a PhD degree whereas a monograph is counted as one book only. For the PhD candidate, writing papers is a way to enter into

the scientific community. On the other hand, a monograph offers a chance to develop an argument thoroughly which articles rarely do. Hence, the term 'compromise'. We did not carry out a separate investigation of what the candidates want, nor what the supervisors advise them to do.

4. We are grateful to each and every one of the institutions we visited.

References

Ag, Astrid, 'Culture as Idea and Practice in Youth and Family Life', PhD dissertation, University of Copenhagen, Copenhagen, 2018, <https://static-curis.ku.dk/portal/files/196716761/Ph.d._afhandling_2018_Ag.PDF>.

Agazzi, Birgitta, Catharina Grünbaum, Rikke Hauge, and Mikael Reuter, *Guldtavlorna i gräset. Nordiskt språksamarbete, historik och framåtblick* (Stockholm: Institutet för Språk och Folkminnen, 2014), <https://www.sprakochfolkminnen.se/download/18.41318b8514835190952928/1529494369354/Guldtavlorna%20r%C3 %A4ttad%20version.pdf>.

Airey, John, 'Can You Teach It in English? Aspects of the Language Choice Debate in Swedish Higher Education', in Robert Wilkinson, ed., *Integrating Content and Language: Meeting the Challenge of a Multilingual Higher Education* (Maastricht: Universitaire Pers, 2004). 97–107.

Bergløv, Emil, '28 % af serene af SKAM er fra Danmark', *Politiken* (20 October 2016), <https://politiken.dk/kultur/filmogtv/article5647726.ece>.

Boyd, Sally and Leena Huss, 'Språkplanering för sveenska i Sverige: Några kritiska Synpunkter', *Sprogforum* 29 (2004), 42–47.

Brink, Eva Theilgaard, *Man skal bare kaste sig ud i det .... En interviewundersøgelse af unge i Nordens nabosprogforståelse i praksis* (Copenhagen: Nordisk Ministerråd, Kulturministeriet, Nordisk Sprogkoordination, 2016).

Börestam, Ulla, *Samma skjorta—olika knappar. Icke-nordiska andraspråkstalares erfarenheter av dansk-svensk språkgemenskap i Öresundsregionen* (Copenhagen: Nordisk Ministerråd, TemaNord 2008:535).

Delsing, Lars-Olof and Katarina Lundin Åkesson, *Håller språket ihop Norden? En forskningsrapport om ungdomars förståelse av danska, svenska och norska* (Copenhagen: Nordisk Ministerråd, TemaNord 2005:573).

Gregersen, Frans et al., *More Parallel, Please! Best Practice of Parallel Language at Nordic Universities: 11 recommendations* (Copenhagen: Nordic Council of Ministers, 2018), <http://norden.diva-portal.org/smash/get/diva2:1203291/FULLTEXT01.pdf>.

Haugen, Einar, 'Nordiske språkproblemer – en opinionsundersökelse', *Nordisk Tidsskrift för vetenskap, konst och industri utgiven av Letterstedtska Föreningen* 29 (1953), 225–249.

Haugen, Einar, 'Semicommunication: The Language Gap in Scandinavian', *Sociological Inquiry* (1966); reprinted with author's comments in Einar Haugen, *Studies by Einar Haugen: Presented on the Occasion of his 65th Birthday April 19 1971* (De Gruyter, 1972), 479–495.

Hult, Francis M., 'English on the Streets of Sweden. An Ecolinguistic View of Two Cities and a Language Policy', *Working Papers in Eudcational Linguistics (WPEL)* 19/1 (2003), 43–63.

Hultgren, Anna-Kristina, Frans Gregersen, and Jacob Thøgersen, 'English at Nordic universities: Ideologies and practices', in Anna-Kristina Hultgren, Frans Gregersen, and Jacob Thøgersen, eds, *English in Nordic Universities. Ideologies and practices* [vol. iv of *Studies in World Language Problems*] (Amsterdam: John Benjamins, 2014), 1–26.

Karker, Allan, 'Nordisk retskrivning—den ideale fordring', *Sprog i Norden* (1976), 39–84.

Kirchmeier, Sabine and Eva Skafte Jensen, 'Nordisk sprogforståelse og kommunikationsstrategier', *Sprog i Norden* (2016), 61–78.

Kirchmeier-Andersen, Sabine, 'Language Use in University Teaching and Research in Denmark', in Gerhard Stickel and Cecilia Robustelli, eds, *Language Use in University Teaching and Research* [band 109 of *Duisburger Arbeiten zur Sprach- under Kulturwissenschaft*] (Frankfurt am Main: Peter Lang, 2015), 145–159.

Kvaran, Gudrún, 'The Use of Foreign Languages at Icelandic Universities', in Gerhard Stickel and Cecilia Robustelli, eds, *Language Use in University Teaching and Research* [band 109 of *Duisburger Arbeiten zur Sprach- under Kulturwissenschaft*] (Frankfurt am Main: Peter Lang, 2015), 137–143.

Ljosland, Ragnhild, 'Language Planning Confronted by Everyday Communication in the International University: The Norwegian Case', *Journal of Multilingual and Multicultural Development* 35/4 (2014), 392–405.

Lund, Sonja Barfod, 'Interskandinaviske interaktioner i et historisk og nutidigt perspektiv', *Globe: A Journal of Language, Culture and Communication* 8 (2019), 34–56.

Maurud, Øivind, *Nabospråksforståelse i Skandinavia. En undersøkelse om gjensidig forståelse av tale- og skriftspråk i Danmark, Norge og Sverige* [Nordisk utredningsserie 13] (Stockholm: Nordiska Rådet, 1975).

Mål i Mun—Förslag till handlingsprogram för svenska språket (Stockholm: Betänkande av Kommittén för svenska språket, SOU 2002:27).

Nordic Council of Ministers, *The Helsinki Treaty. Treaty of Co-operation between Denmark, Finland, Iceland, Norway and Sweden* (Copenhagen: Nordic Council of Ministers, ANP 2018:746), <http://norden.diva-portal.org/smash/get/diva2:1250815/FULLTEXT01.pdf>.

Nordisk Ministerråd, *Deklararation om nordisk språkpolitik* (Copenhagen: Nordisk Ministerråd, ANP 2007: 746), <http://norden.divaportal.org/smash/get/diva2:700895/FULLTEXT01.pdf>.

Ohlsson, Stig Örjan, *Nordisk språkförståelse—i går, i dag, i morgon. Nordisk radio och television via satellit. Kultur- och programpolitisk delrapport* [band 3, bilaga 6 of *NU A*] (Stockholm, Nordiska ministerrådet, 1979).

Ohlsson, Stig Örjan, 'anmeldelse af Einar Haugen: The Scandinavian Languages'. *Danske Studier* (1978a).

Ohlsson, Stig Örjan, 'Nordisk språkhistoria och nordisk språkvård', *Språk i Norden* (1978b), 17–40.

Östman, Jan-Ola, 'Language Use in Academia in the Nordic Countries—With Special Reference to Finland', in Gerhard Stickel and Cecilia Robustelli, eds, *Language Use in University Teaching and Research* [band 109 of *Duisburger Arbeiten zur Sprach- under Kulturwissenschaft*] (Frankfurt am Main: Peter Lang, 2015), 85–98.

Quist, Pia and Astrid Ravn Skovse, 'Sprog i og uden om SKAM: autenticitets-element, fællesskabsmarkør og vare', *Nordisk Tidsskrift for Informationsvidenskab og Kulturformidling* 2/3 (2017), 43–53.

Quist, Pia and Bente Ailin Svendsen, eds, *Multilingual Urban Scandinavia. New Linguistic Practices* (Bristol/Buffalo/Toronto: Multingual Matters, 2017).

Soler, Josep, *Language Policy and the Internationalization of Universities. A Focus on Estonian Higher Education* [vol xv of *Language and Social Life*] (Berlin/Boston: De Gruyter Mouton, 2019).

Söderlundh, Hedda, 'Global Policies and Local Norms: Sociolinguistic Awareness and Language Choice at an International University', *International Journal of the Sociology of Language* 216 (2012), 87–109.

Teleman, Ulf and Margareta Westman, 'Behöver Sverige en nationell språkpolitik?', *Språkvård* 2 (1997), 5–16.

Wright, Sue, *Language Policy and Language Planning* (London: Palgrave Macmillan, 2016).

Part III Languages in Postcolonial Regions

Hermann Giliomee

The Rise and Fall of Afrikaans-medium Universities[1]

The rise of Afrikaans-medium universities between 1917 and 1967 was closely associated with the rapid development of Afrikaans in the course of the twentieth century from a spoken language without much status attached to it to a well-developed formal language used in all public functions, including postgraduate studies. By the late 1980s there were six Afrikaans-medium universities. Between 1990 and 2015 Afrikaans suffered a precipitous decline. At present only one of the 24 universities in South Africa uses Afrikaans as the main medium of instruction and it is done in only one of its three campuses. As black students filled the classes of the previously 'liberal' universities, many white English-language students fled to the traditionally Afrikaans universities. Once they formed more than roughly a quarter of the student body, they started to insist on English-medium instruction. They were joined by black students who tend to project Afrikaans as the language of apartheid. University authorities try to defend the switch from Afrikaans to English as part of their project to improve the university's ranking internationally. This chapter discusses both the rise and possible demise of Afrikaans as a public language with special reference to universities.

Keywords: Afrikaans, higher education, language policy, universities

Introduction

In 1977 a German linguist observed that of all the non-European/non-Asiatic languages, Afrikaans is the only one that in the twentieth century gained full university status and came to be used in all branches of life and learning. Only Hindi, Indonesian and Hebrew matched the rise of Afrikaans from a colloquial language to one used in all walks of life, including at both undergraduate and graduate level at university (Kloss 1977, p. 10).

By the early 1970s there were five Afrikaans-medium universities for white people and one for coloured people. An astute analyst considered it the strongest language in South Africa in the way it was being used formally and informally in all contexts as a first or second language (cited in Giliomee et al., 2001, p. 117).

But since the regime change in 1994 Afrikaans-medium instruction at the Historically Afrikaans Universities (HAUs) has suffered great blows. It is now an open question if Afrikaans can survive as a literary and intellectual language. University education is today virtually entirely in English, although only 2.9 % of the black population speak the language as a first language. Afrikaans speakers form the third largest language community in South Africa, as the language is spoken by three-quarters of the coloured people, three-fifths of the white population, 5 % of Asians and 1.5 % of black people (Lehohla 2012[2]).

In the Western Cape province 75.6 % of the schools are Afrikaans-medium. Yet none of the four universities in the province make a significant offer in Afrikaans. A full offer in Afrikaans-medium instruction is made only at one of the 37 campuses in the country.

Afrikaans-medium schools produce more than enough good candidates for Afrikaans-medium universities. By 2017 white Afrikaans-speaking pupils made up 21 % of all pupils with university exemption. Afrikaans schools produced a third of all the matric pupils who passed mathematics with distinction. Just over 73,000 out of a present student population of more than a million are Afrikaans-speaking (Flip Smit cited in *Beeld* 2017, 2018a).

NB Publishers, which is part of the Naspers conglomerate, is the largest publisher in the country. In 2014 the Afrikaans share of all the books books sold in the country had risen to 49 %. The ten top-selling fiction titles were all in Afrikaans, as were the top children books. Turnover in sales in the period 2004–14 increased by 25 % (Stassen 2016). The number of Afrikaans books in print has risen from 5,000 to 8,500.

The Rise of Afrikaans-medium Universities

By 1900 Afrikaans was spoken across South Africa, but it had virtually no literature of any merit. After the South African War (1899–1902), in which Great Britain defeated the Boer republics, English appeared destined to become the sole official language. However, in the constitutional negotiations it became clear that if economic growth was to be rekindled, reconciliation between the two white communities was of primary importance. The choice fell on granting effective equal status to English and Dutch as the official languages of the new state. In 1925 Afrikaans became an official language, and would soon replace Dutch.

Giving expression to the constitutional commitment to bilingualism, the Government in 1918 established Stellenbosch University (SU), which would soon become an Afrikaans-medium institution, and the University of Cape Town (UCT), which was an English-medium university. Subsequently the University of Witwatersrand (Wits), the University of Natal, and Rhodes University were founded as English-medium universities. At UCT and Wits there was a modest poportion of students who were not white, but the other English-medium universities remained segregated until the 1970s.

In 1932 the University of Pretoria (UP) became the second Afrikaans-medium university. Three more Afrikaans single-medium universities were later founded: the University of the Orange Free State (UOFS) in 1950, Potchefstroom University (PU) in 1951, and the Rand Afrikaans University (RAU) in 1968 in Johannesburg. After 1994 these universities together with SU came to be known as the HAUs.

In 1964 the University of Port Elizabeth opened its doors as a dual-medium university. The University of South Africa provided distance education to all people in Afrikaans and English.

In 1959 the Government passed a law that provided for the founding of several segregated university colleges for blacks in the so-called 'homelands'. It also established a university college in Durban for Indians with English as medium of instruction and also one in Cape Town for coloured people. The latter, which initially used Afrikaans as medium of instruction, gained university status in 1970 as the University of Western Cape (UWC). The other colleges founded in terms of the 1959 legislation also became universities.

A Medium of Scientific Communication

The Afrikaner community only urbanized on a large scale during the first four decades of the twentieth century. Many of the newly urbanized lacked skills and a good command of both English and Dutch. In the early 1930s a commission found that a quarter of the white population, most of whom were Afrikaners, was desperately poor. It became a matter of urgency to develop Afrikaans as a medium of instruction both at school and university to combat large-scale Afrikaner poverty.

At the same time many of the better educated Afrikaners used Afrikaans as a badge of their new ethnic identity. Shortly after the unification of South Africa in 1910, John X. Merriman, a leading liberal in the first two decades of Union, expressed a negative view of these efforts. He wrote to the historian W.M. Macmillan: "Afrikaans, which is so sedulously inculcated as a point of honour, acts as a fearful clog on the poor wretches who have to earn their living in towns or with large industrial employers who are generally English-speaking" (Macmillan 1975, p. 134).

For the first 60 years of the Union, lecturers at the Afrikaans universities focused heavily on teaching in order to help their students, most of whom struggled to master the English textbooks. But the Afrikaans universities did not only teach. Afrikaans steadily acquired an academic literature, offering an intellectual paradigm that differed from the one that had originated in Britain and was spread locally by the English universities.

Legal scholars stressed the importance of Roman-Dutch law, initially irritating their English colleagues. who wanted to focus only on English law. In 1937 the *Tydskrif vir Romeins-Hollandse Reg* (*Journal for Roman-Dutch Law*) appeared for the first time. With growing numbers of Afrikaner lawyers being appointed to the bench, the influence of Roman-Dutch law on jurisprudence steadily increased. J.C. de Wet, professor of law at SU, published pathbreaking works especially on the law of contracts (1947) and criminal law (1949).

The earliest historians who wrote in Afrikaans were nationalist historians who took up the cudgels against the colonial school of history that glorified British rule in South Africa. During the 1930s the first academically trained Afrikaner historians started to publish. They challenged both the liberal and Marxist schools of English South Africans, who were mostly influenced by the British emphasis on individual rights and the material interests of either individuals or classes. Afrikaner historians emphasized the influence of culture, and argued that it affects history as much as material interests do.

In 2018 Mahmood Mamdani, an esteemed African-born intellectual, deplored the policy of African states to embrace the colonial language as medium of instruction in schools and universities, while also failing to develop their own languages and intellectual traditions. The Afrikaners, he argued, represent the complete opposite. He stated: "[Afrikaans] represents the most successful decolonising initiative on the African continent, having developed from a folkloric language to being the bearer of an intellectual tradition in less than half a century" (cited in *Beeld* 2018b).

After the Second World War there was a constant increase in the number of scientific articles published in Afrikaans. In 1980 Afrikaans was the 32nd language in frequency in the titles of articles indexed by *Chemical Abstracts* (more than those in Hindi, Armenian and Arabic). It was 25th in *Index Medicus* (Laponce 1987, p. 72–3).

In the final quarter of the twentieth century English began to expand rapidly in the Western world as the dominant language of dissertations and of scientific publications. At South African universities the Afrikaans share of dissertations written in the humanities and social sciences between 1975 and 1996 dropped from 62 % to 48 %. In the natural sciences it slumped from 36 % to 9 %.

In law journals the Afrikaans share had fallen below a third by 1996–97. It was even lower in several other academic journals, such as *SA Journal of Philosophy* (6 %), *SA Journal of Psychology* (6 %), *SA Journal of Economics* (1 %), and *SA Journal of Higher Education* (16 %) (research by Ponelis and Mouton cited in Giliomee and Schlemmer 2006, p. 159–63).

By the 1980s, peer evaluation and ratings of both individual researchers and universities had become an increasingly important criterion for universities. In 1981 Erich Reynhardt, a physicist at the the University of South Africa, published an article in which he compared the research productivity of South African universities to a sample of European unversities. He focused on articles published during the 1970s in academic journals in physics, chemistry and mathematical sciences. He found that academics in South Africa were less productive than their European counterparts and that in South Africa the English universities outperformed their Afrikaans counterparts.

Reynhardt also calculated the number of years/researcher per publication. The UCT came first, with researchers taking 1.4 years per article, followed by Wits and UOFS at 1.9, PU at 3.2, and SU way behind at 5.9 (Vaughan 2015, p. 77). Alarmed, the Council for Scientific and Industrial Research, the premier research organisation in the natural sciences and engineering, approached Jack de Wet, a highly rated mathematician and a fellow of Balliol College in Oxford. He was asked to investigate the state of research in the faculties of natural sciences and engineering in South African universities and make recommendations to improve it.

The report introduced a five-tier system of ratings of researchers based on a track-record evaluation of them by their peers. In de Wet's system category A was reserved for researchers who without any doubt were internationally accepted as leaders in their respective fields; B for people who enjoyed considerabe respect but were not quite at the very top; C for researchers who showed steady productivity and who were published abroad. The current rating system of reseachers by the National Research Foundation (NRF) is based on de Wet's system.

The table was topped by the four English-medium universities, all scoring a good overall mark. At the top university, there were 13 A-grades, 33 B-grades and 50 C-grades. SU was at the very bottom with no scholar with an A-grade, three B-grades and 10 C-grades. UP and Potchefstroom were slightly above this score (Botha 2018, p. 221). The UOFS scored a mediocre overall mark, halfway between the Afrikaans-medium universities at the bottom and the English-medium universities at the top (Vaughan 2015, p. 77–8). Most of the researchers in the top categories published in English and did so mostly in international journals. Early in the twenty-first century the rating system was extended to the humanities and social sciences and subsequently to other faculties.

De Wet's report and the rating system were a major wake-up call for the Afrikaans universities, and particularly for SU. From its inception SU had seen itself as the university that led and set the tone for all other Afrikaans-medium tertiary education institutions. In 1943 (Stellenbosch Student) the editor of a SU student magazine wrote: "Whether we would like to admit or not we are highly pleased with ourselves. Is SU not the cradle of Afrikanerdom?" This sense of self-importance was bolstered by the fact that five of the eight prime ministers and presidents between 1910 and 1994 were SU alumni. In 1962, ten of the eighteen cabinet ministers and 36 of the members of Parliament were SU alumni (Grundlingh 2018, p. 34).

From the late 1980s SU's academic performance steadily improved and so did its position on the ratings tables. But in its zeal to improve its academic image, SU would increasingly discard the task of transferring the Afrikaans language and culture through teaching in Afrikaans and supporting journals that published research in Afrikaans. Facing no Afrikaans competition in the southern part of the country, SU increasingly took a free rider position with respect to Afrikaans after the 1980s.

Flip Smit (pers. comm.), an SU alumnus who served as vice-chancellor of the University of Pretoria during the 1990s, provides the following acute observation:

> The scars of the scientific isolation of universities in the apartheid era ran deep. Especially the ex-Afrikaans universities fell over their feet to embrace internationalisation. Perhaps that is why they went overboard in their attempts to climb in the ranking system and thus demonstrate that their institution was on its way to achieving international status.[3]

Afrikaans as the medium of communicating research in the country declined steadily. Between 1991 and 1997 only 15 % of the natural sciences doctoral degree dissertations accepted were written in Afrikaans; for the humanities and social sciences the figure was 36 %. Half the academic articles published by academics attached to the social sciences were written in Afrikaans; it was down to a third by 2007 (Ponelis 1999). There were the following reasons for the decline (Ponelis 1999):

- The great strength of English locally and abroad as a *lingua franca*
- The stigma imparted by attempts to give apartheid and nationalism scientific credibility
- The job market
- The new political order

To improve its rankings and also to receive more revenue generated by state subsidies for publications, SU embarked on a concerted effort to recruit top-level researchers to Stellenbosch. Most of them were English speakers who would not have normally applied for a post at an Afrikaans university. SU offered to release them from the obligation to become proficient in Afrikaans in order to get tenure and did not require most of them to teach undergraduates. This helped SU to start climbing steadily in the rankings. However, firm rules remained in force until early in the twenty-first century. There was no question of other lecturers openly bending the rules and giving their lectures in English or largely in English, which would increasingly happen after 2002.

From 2002 many more lecturers would be appointed that would use English in their undergraduate lectures. Almost all promised to learn Afrikaans but the rule that profiency in Afrikaans was a prerequisite for a permanent appointment tacitly fell away. SU justified the switch to English as a prerequisite for rising strongly in the national and international rankings.

By 2017, SU was the institution where most master's and doctoral degrees were awarded in relation to its size. Yet it was not performing particularly well if measured by the accredited publications of its staff. In the official statistics for 2017, published by the Department of Higher Education, books, publications in journals and published conference proceedings are tallied to produce a log. The University of Pretoria topped the log with a total of 2,062.94 units, followed by the University of KwaZulu-Natal, and the University of Witwatersrand. Stellenbosch came fourth with 1,882.63 units (Rapport 2018, p. 2). It must be taken into account that UP's staff is larger than that of SU. It is generally accepted that, when calculated per capita, SU's academic staff members are the most productive in the country.

But rising in the international rankings was a much tougher challenge. The Centre for World University Rankings for the years 2015 to 2017 shows all the top South African universities falling by twenty points or more: Wits to 176th, UCT to 265th, SU to 329th, and UP to 697th. In the Times Higher Education World University Rankings for 2019, Stellenbosch University came third among the South African universities after the University of Cape Town and Witwatersrand University. Recently Philip Altbach and Ellen Hazelkorn argued that the ranking system perverts the true function of the university, namely to transfer the knowledge and skills the graduates would need in the communities that they would one day serve (Altbach and Hazelkorn 2017).

De Wet's rating system tends to favour established areas of research, and established informal research networks. The danger exists of a relatively small number of reviewers carrying disproportionate weight (Fedderke 2013).

Decline as Medium of Instruction

The main reasons for the sharp decline of Afrikaans are the following.

A Dramatic Increase of Black and Coloured Student Numbers

Firstly there were dramatic increases in the number of students from communities which are not white. This is shown in Table 6.1.

Table 6.1: Student Population Figures

	BLACK STUDENTS	COLOURED STUDENTS	INDIAN STUDENTS	WHITE STUDENTS	TOTAL
1986	54,997	13,552	21,838	177,744	277,115
2014	679,800	60,716	53,611	166,172	969,154
2018	763,767	64,772	50,131	148,802	1,036,984[4]

Source: HEMIS (Higher Education Management Information System)

Between 1986 and 2018 the number of black students increased fourteen times and that of coloured students five times. With strong teacher unions blocking reform, particularly the introduction of school inspectors, the quality of entrants from predominantly black state schools failed to improve markedly.

The Children's Institute at University of Cape Town reported in 2015 that the underachievement of black children at school is such that by the end of secondary school they are at least five years behind their "privileged counterparts" (De Lannoy et al., 2015). In 2016 South Africa's Statistician General, Pali Lehohla, in presenting to Parliament statistics for higher education expressed his horror about the failure rate of blacks. They had been taught in their second language, while whites had generally received mother-tongue instruction. Lehohla said that during the 1980s for every black graduate there were 1.2 white graduates. In 2015, for every one black person who graduated from university, there were six white students who made it through successfully. He declared these figures "a horror" that was totally unacceptable (Gqirani 2016).

Flights to Afrikaans-medium Universities

Table 6.2 gives the shrinking proportion in 2017 of Afrikaans students at HAUs and the Cape Peninsula University of Technology (CPUT), which on one of its campuses trains teachers for Afrikaans primary schools in the coloured community.

Two separate flights of students put great pressure on Afrikaans as a medium of instruction. First, growing numbers of blacks turned their backs on the black 'homeland' universities and sought admission to one of the predominantly white universities. Another flight was that of white and coloured students, who turned away from the old English universities in order to enroll at the HAUs, either because they were not admitted to an English university or because they considered the HAUs as safer and better managed. As their numbers in a class grew beyond the tipping point, commonly assumed to be somewhere between a

Table 6.2: Student Enrolment: Afrikaans Home Language

INSTITUTION	INSTITUTION DESCRIPTION	2005	2009	2012	2015	2017
US	University of Stellenbosch	60 %	53 %	51 %	42 %	38 %
UNW	North-West University	34 %	31 %	30 %	28 %	28 %
UP	University of Pretoria	36 %	29 %	29 %	24 %	22 %
UFS	University of the Free State	33 %	31 %	26 %	25 %	19 %
CPUT	Cape Peninsula University of Technology	22 %	20 %	19 %	17 %	15 %
NATIONAL		15 %	13 %	12 %	10 %	9 %

Source: HEMIS (Higher Education Management Information System)

quarter and a third of the class, they invariably started to demand that part of the lecture be presented in English. By the year 2000 students with Afrikaans as their home language made up only 56 % of all the students at the HAUs.

This created a very difficult situation for the HAUs, which had to contend with a government that from the start had provided no extra funding for parallel-medium instruction but nevertheless insisted on access for blacks through being not only admitted but also taught in English. Many lecturers were unwilling to give their lectures in both Afrikaans and English without extra compensation.

The process of displacement of Afrikaans started at the University of the Western Cape in the early 1970s when large numbers of black students coming from the Eastern Cape enrolled. They forced UWC to replace Afrikaans with English as the medium of instruction. In the course of the 1980s Afrikaans was steadily diminished due to a radical change in the composition of the student body. By 2005 there were approximately 14,000 students at UWC. Afrikaans-speakers formed only 17 % of the total, 33 % spoke an indigenous African language as their first language, while 45 % indicated that English was their first or preferred language.

Jaap Durand (pers. comm.), deputy vice-chancellor at UWC, recounts: "The academic performance of our brown students declined markedly after Afrikaans as a medium was dropped. In retrospect I would say that the brown Afrikaans-speaking students were significantly disadvantaged as a result of our decision."[5]

Coloured Afrikaans speakers at present have the lowest rate of participation in university education and the lowest throughput rate. It is generally accepted that the main cause is the dominance of English as medium of instruction at UWC and other universities.

At present, most coloured Afrikaans-speaking pupils attend English-medium high schools. Afrikaans is still widely used in coloured primary schools and teachers for these schools are trained in the medium of Afrikaans at the Wellington campus of CPUT. They formed 22 % of the student population in 2005 but this has declined to 15 % in 2017 (see Table 6.2).

RAU in Johannesburg was the first of the HAUs where Afrikaans was terminated as a medium of instruction. From the early 1990s white and black students who wished to be taught in English enrolled in large numbers. Afrikaans-speaking undergraduates at its Auckland Park campus dropped from 33 % of the total student population in 1995 to 15 % in 2005 (Giliomee and Schlemmer 2006, p. 89). In this year the Government forced the issue by compelling RAU to merge with Vista University and Wits Technikon, two English-medium tertiary education institutions. It renamed the institution the University of Johannesburg. Instruction in Afrikaans was terminated.

At the University of Port Elizabeth a form of parallel-medium instruction was used effectively until the mid-1980s, when large numbers of black students began to enroll. In the late 1990s the university abruptly ended all tuition in Afrikaans without giving any notice (Hill 2009). A lecturer (pers. comm.) made a wry comment: "To the best of my knowledge the transition to single English-medium never took place: it is a creeping disease that no one ever admits suffering from, like leprosy or Alzheimer."[6] In 2004, the University of Port Elizabeth was renamed Nelson Mandela Metropolitan University.

Turning to the HAUs, one is struck by the major difference the person at the helm of the university management made to preserving Afrikaans as an academic language. There were three vice-chancellors over the past two decades who distinguished themselves with creative responses to the twin challenges of promoting the greater good of society and preserving as much as possible of Afrikaans. They were Francois Retief at the University of the Free State (1988–1997), Andreas van Wyk at Stellenbosch University (1993–2001) and Theuns Eloff at North-West University (2004–14). The former two will receive attention later in this contribution, the latter's efforts follow now.

In 2004 the Government established North-West University as a multi-campus university that incorporated PU, a university in Mahikeng and the Vaal Triangle Technicon. The former two were located in the North-West province and the latter in the Gauteng province. Theuns Eloff, who became the first vice-chancellor after the merger, played an innovative role in retaining Afrikaans-medium instruction on the Potchefstroom campus. On a visit to Brussels, Eloff took special note of the extensive system of interpretation taking place in the meetings of the European Community. On his return, his proposal was accepted that at the Potchefstroom campus the language of instruction continued to be Afrikaans but with simultaneous translation from Afrikaans to English being offered.

Under the system all students are obliged to pass a language proficiency test either in English or Afrikaans. A special office handles complaints about the practical implementation of the language policy. Lecturers are encouraged to publish some of their work in Afrikaans. Potchefstroom lecturers make the biggest contribution (about a third) to articles that appear in Afrikaans in academic journals.

An Ambiguous Constitution

Article 29(2) of South Africa's Constitution extends to citizens "the right to receive education in the official language or languages of their choice in public educational institutions where that education is reasonably practicable." But there is also an equality clause that stipulates that "everyone is equal before the law and has the right to equal protection and benefit of the law." During the 1990s no one thought that a court would use the latter clause as one of the justifications to exclude Afrikaans as a medium of instruction.

In 1993, at a late stage of the negotiations for an interim constitution, Piet Marais, the last Minister of National Education of the National Party (NP), warned (then still) President Frederik Willem de Klerk that "education was not a priority among the NP negotiators." He added that in informal talks with some negotiators of African National Congress (ANC) he had gained the clear impression that they "displayed an intolerance towards Afrikaans and to the demand that the Afrikaans universities could continue to imbue their mission with a cultural content" (pers. comm.).[7]

The issue of the medium of instruction nearly caused a breakdown in the negotiations for the constitution that took place in 1995 and 1996. Cyril Ramaphosa, chairperson of the Constitutional Assembly, pointed out that the NP negotiators had left him in the dark over the importance their party attached to education.[8] In the negotiations the NP and the ANC deferred the resolution of contentious issues to the new government. There was no clarity about what was meant by negotiations or agreement. The NP thought that deals struck could change only by mutual agreement. The ANC, by contrast, fought a classic 'war of position' in which each concession it extracted from the Government became the platform for the next assault (see African National Congress 1992; du Toit 2000). No attempt was made to spell out how potential conflicts were to be resolved.

The Government of National Unity, in which both Nelson Mandela and de Klerk served, broke down in 1996. The NP's voters deserted the party in droves and the party disbanded in 2004. No longer constrained by any opposition party, the ANC took aim at the HAUs. None of the old English universities were forced to merge with other universities, but three of the HAUs were forced into mergers that made little sense in academic terms. By 2016, the ANC Government targeted the right of Afrikaans speakers to receive education in Afrikaans if a similar right was not extended to speakers of other African languages.

Disunity Among the HAUs

In 1992, Stellenbosch University had Parliament pass a law stipulating that Afrikaans is its medium of instruction. In 1996 Stellenbosch University (see *Address*) was first of the HAUs to offer Mandela an honorary degree. In his acceptance speech he said: "Within a system comprising more than twenty universities, surely it must be possible to reach an accommodation to the effect that there will be at least one university whose main tasks will include that of seeing to the sustained development of Afrikaans as an academic medium."

Jakes Gerwel, an former vice-chancellor of UWC and Director-General in the President's office, warned SU management privately that it had to negotiate the right to teach mainly in Afrikaans with the new government and with the other HAUs. There the matter rested until 2001 when Gerwel launched an initiative. He invited the five vice-chancellors of the HAUs to a meeting where he proposed a system in which Afrikaans would enjoy a secure place in at least two universities. These universities would be obliged to report to Parliament annually on the way in which they performed this function.

The vice-chancellors of SU and PU were willing to accept the opportunity but the three other vice-chancellors were determined to keep their Afrikaans students. They objected so strenuously that Gerwel's plan had to be dropped. A golden opportunity was lost. Every vice-chancellor looked only after his own university's interests. At that point UP had more than 16,000 Afrikaans students enrolled. No vice-chancellor would easily lose much of that market.

In 2002 the Department of Higher Education and Training (DHET) published its 'Language Policy for Higher Education', which is still on the books. It is a double-edged document. On the one hand it rejects the demand that non-Afrikaans speakers had to acquire proficiency in Afrikaans if they wish to study at one of the HAUs. It states: "While it could be argued that such a requirement in the case of foreign students is reasonable, requiring the same of South African students constitutes an unjust imposition and additional burden of demand." This ignores the fact that a large number of blacks passed Afrikaans Higher in the final year of school, which should enable them to study in Afrikaans. On the other hand the policy pledges its full support for the retention of Afrikaans as a medium of communication and commits itself to ensuring that the capacity of Afrikaans to function as a medium is not eroded. It also endorses the development of the other African languages in the country (Ministry of Education 2002).

Yet there has been no attempt to provide funding for parallel-medium to realize these objectives. The DHET does not require universities to report on how multilingualism is implemented and neither is there any empirical measurement. In 2016, Niek Grové (p. 3), who was a professor of law and served as UP registrar from 2000 to 2017, wrote:

> In my opinion the DHET did not act in good faith. It stood back and allowed the language traditions of our country to become diluted and downscaled. […] Thus far the DHET has failed to act in promotion of the indigenous languages—both Afrikaans and other indigenous languages.

The Courts' Opposition to Parallel-Medium

The crucial test for Afrikaans as a university language would take place at the University of Pretoria and Stellenbosch University which enrolled the most Afrikaans students. Under Smit, vice-chancellor from 1992 to 1996, UP was defined as an Afrikaans university that also offered classes in the medium of English if student numbers and classroom space allowed it. Smit was succeeded by Johan van Zyl. For him Afrikaans could remain as a language of instruction but only if the market indicated that enough students demanded it. In large classes parallel-medium was used, but in small classes lecturers could give part of the lecture in Afrikaans and the other part in English. By 2005, senior office bearers observed that in the latter case the use of English predominated. Lecturers were not required to be proficient in both media of instruction.

Vic Webb, director of language policy at UP, stated that in a reasonably short period the position of Afrikaans had declined from one in which the UP's statute laid down that it was the only language of instruction to one where it was "barely tolerated" (Giliomee and Schlemmer 2006, p. 93–102). As a result of the large intake of non-Afrikaans students the proportion of students who preferred instruction in Afrikaans shrunk fast, as is shown in Table 6.3.

In 2010 UP once again committed itself to Afrikaans as the language of instruction. One of the most important recommendations was that certain core undergaduate programmes and modules would be presented in both English and

Table 6.3: Proportion of UP Students Preferring Afrikaans

1995	1999	2004	2010	2015
71 %	59 %	44 %	38 %	18 %

Source: UP Figures

Afrikaans, along with a large number of programmes that would be presented in English only.

This policy was challenged in court on the grounds that it granted Afrikaans-speaking students a privilege that was not extended to speakers of other African languages. The court ruled in favour of English as the only medium of instruction. It conceded that the policy favoured the small proportion of whites whose home language was English, but argued that the Afrikaans-speaking students are known to be reasonably proficient in English as a second language. If they were put in a position where some of their courses are in Afrikaans, they would enjoy a "pedagogic advantage" over blacks that was unfair.[9]

The ruling was made regardless of the fact that speakers of African languages in the northern provinces have not made any progress in developing their language to a point where it can be used as a medium of instruction at university level. It was a strange judgement, showing the extent to which the courts have come to the view that, except for English, all the official languages as media of instruction have to be treated on the basis of absolute equality.

The University of the Free State (UFS) was well prepared for the new political order under Francois Retief who served as vice-chancellor from 1988 to 1997. He first won the staff's support for a properly planned and firmly applied policy of parallel-medium. It gave a key role to an ombudsperson who regularly inquired from department heads whether policy was being applied fairly. Any deviation had to be submitted to the university's executive. Lecturers had to demonstrate their proficiency in the language in which they gave lectures. Students too had to pass a language proficiency test. The university made extensive use of the services of translators and interpreters, used at virtually all meetings and lectures. Members of the UFS executive interviewed in 2006 rebutted objections to parallel-medium instruction often raised at other HAUs. In their view the system was not "excessively expensive" and while it did initially negatively affect research productivity, output recovered after a short spell (Giliomee and Schlemmer 2006, p. 77–82).

With determined leadership, like that shown by Retief, Afrikaans could survive. This possibility was destroyed in 2009 when Jonathan Jansen was appointed as vice-chancellor. At that point there were—according to UFS figures—8,738 Afrikaans-speaking students, 4,379 with English as home language, 15,847 who spoke a South African Bantu language as their first language, and 3,198 listed as 'other'. More than 90 % of the Afrikaans-speaking students attended the lectures presented in Afrikaans at the university's Bloemfontein campus (Du Plessis 2010, p. 13).

In 2009 Stanford University published Jansen's book called *Confronting Race and the Apartheid Past*. Jansen argued that the best solution for the crisis in public education in South Africa was to abolish Afrikaans from the first school day and instead teach all children in the medium of English. In Jansen's view racism was transmitted from one Afrikaner generation to another in Afrikaans-medium educational institutions, constituting a serious threat to social cohesion in South Africa.

Afrikaans survived at UFS in a parallel-medium structure until 2016 when the Afrikaans stream was abolished. The university made the unsubstantiated claim that parallel-medium instruction promoted racism. The Constitutional Court concurred despite a lack of evidence leading to that effect. It also ignored the result of the only opinion poll, conducted in 2015, that found that more than 60 % of the students at the Bloemfontein campus of UFS favoured parallel-medium instruction (Steyn 2016).

Mogoeng Mogoeng, the Chief Justice, backed by the other black judges on the bench (but with the three white judges dissenting), upheld the university's decision to abolish Afrikaans as a medium of instruction in almost all faculties. He argued that Afrikaans has "unwittingly become an instrument of racial and cultural division". Apartheid was a "crime against humanity" which had "left us with many scars". Continued use of Afrikaans as a major medium of instruction would leave the results of white supremacy "alive and well". It was not "reasonably practicable" to retain it when race relations were "poisoned thereby".

In a supporting opinion Judge Chris Jafta said that it could not be expected from a transformative constitution to recognize cultural traditions that were racist and oppressive. They had to be discarded in the rubbish bin of history. In his dissenting judgement, supported by two other judges, Judge Johan Froneman pointed out that the university had offered no concrete evidence that Afrikaner students were guilty of discrimination with the exception of a vague reference to "observable incidents" and "empirical research". It would have been better, he argued, to refer the matter back to the Appeal Court, where the matter could be decided on the basis of evidence presented by the university (ZACC 2017, p. 30–47).

De Klerk felt compelled to respond to the judgement and especially to the words of Judge Jafta. He said:

> In hindsight it is clear that the ANC negotiators during the 1990s deliberately misled not only the Afrikaners but all non-ANC parties regarding their intentions in the medium and long term. It had become clear [...] that it was never their intention to honour all the rights incorporated in the Constitution. (de Klerk 2018)

The warning in 1993 of Marais was indeed prescient (see Marais in the section 'An Ambiguous Constitution').

John Kane-Berman (2018), a former chief executive officer of the Institute of Race Relations, the main liberal organisation in civil society, wrote that it did appear as if the Constitutional Court wanted to punish the Afrikaners for ever for the sins of their fathers.

The Abandonment of Cultural Transfer As Part of a Mission in Favour of the Promotion of Corporate Interests

Opponents of the continued use of Afrikaans as a medium of instruction tended to project this as a throwback to the years of NP rule when the Afrikaans universities were subservient to the needs and dictates of the Afrikaner nationalist movement. It became known as the era of the *volksuniversiteit*. But this allegation can be dismissed as anachronistic. The *volksuniversiteit* idea had perished in the 1980s under pressure from the international ratings and rankings. There is no longer any danger that educational institutions would again allow themselves to become the handmaiden of a nationalist movement and ideology. The argument now is that using Afrikaans as a medium of instruction as well as operating within the framework of a liberal constitution can contribute greatly to the fostering of cultural diversity and political tolerance.

During the transition to democracy in the 1990s the use of English on the SU campus became more frequent. Fearing that Afrikaans would be scaled down under a new government, some lecturers began using English in classes in order to attract students who wanted to be taught in English. When informed of this, vice-chancellor Andreas van Wyk immediately warned the department head or lecturer that the university would not allow its language policy to be flouted.

At SU, the election of a new vice-chancellor in 2001 became a contest between two candidates of whom one favoured the emphasis on cultural transmission, whereas the other advocated the promotion of corporate interests. Rolf Stumpf, who was narrowly beaten, declared to Council that the existence and development of SU had been mainly determined by the Afrikaans community. He added: "I have always believed that Stellenbosch should remain an Afrikaans university from a national-diversity perspective. Language coupled with culture are also important considerations for diversity." By contrast Chris Brink, who was appointed, declared that English could be used in a limited way, but that "good management" would ensure that Afrikaans remained the most important medium of instruction (Giliomee and Schlemmer 2006, p. 103–10).

Soon, however, the executive committee of the University Council, under the chairmanship of Edwin Hertzog, along with Brink, began to regard the university as a corporate institution not accountable to any region or community or culture but as mainly driven by its own corporate financial interests. Hertzog and his allies on Council were all businessmen and none of them were elected on the ticket of introducing English on a large scale. They had no public support for their actions. Letters to the local Afrikaans newspaper overwhelmingly supported the policy of SU remaining a predominantly Afrikaans university (Giliomee 2017, p. 293–322).

Koos Bekker (in *Die Burger* 2005), CEO of Naspers, now the largest company in Africa, and a Council member, expressed an opinion that radically clashed with that of Hertzog. He asked three questions: "What kind of community do we want to build in the Western Cape? What is the everyday language in Stellenbosch? Who can Afrikaans rely on?" He added: "If Stellenbosch becomes an English-medium university it chooses in my view the road of cowardice. It turns our backs on our roots in Africa and our brown brothers and sisters."

Brink was elected to the post of vice-chancellor on the back of his promise that Afrikaans would enjoy a secure place at SU on account of his 'good management' of the language issue. Brink tried to manage the language policy without language-proficiency conditions, or rules and supervision. Predictably, it led to the large-scale undermining of Afrikaans. Very few lecturers and students whose command of Afrikaans was deemed to be at risk completed the Afrikaans course at the Language Centre. The head of the Afrikaans Unit wrote: "There is no intrinsic motivation for the non-Afrikaans student to acquire Afrikaans. Everything is made so easy for him or her …" (Giliomee and Schlemmer 2006, p. 256).

The main medium used to reduce Afrikaans to a minimum as a medium of instruction was the so-called T-option (the bilingual option) where both languages were intermittently used in the same class. It amounted to nothing less than a Trojan horse. It made it possible for those whose Afrikaans was poor to sit back and wait for the lecturer to repeat Afrikaans passages in English.

In 2005 SU decided to allow the T-option in the Faculty of Arts and Humanities to be used in all three years of the bachelor's degree. The management presented it in the Council as an 'experiment' that would be conducted over three years. In 2008 it was discovered that no experiment had taken place. To placate the faction in the Council that objected strongly to the rapid shrinking of the Afrikaans offer, it was decided to commission a professional agency to conduct a scientific survey of the language preferences of undergraduate students The survey found that more than 80 % of the Afrikaans-speaking respondents and more than 40 % of English-speaking respondents preferred mainly Afrikaans-medium instruction. More respondents preferred parallel-medium than the T-option (Schlemmer 2008). The survey pointed to the need for SU to revert to Afrikaans as the main medium of instruction or introducing parallel-medium instruction. It could also have stepped up efforts to attract more coloured Afrikaans-speaking students.

Instead the SU management greatly increased the recruitment of students who preferred English-medium instruction, as Table 6.4 shows. It was almost as if SU wanted to put facts on the ground that would make the predominant position of English unassailable. As Table 6.4 indicates the language profile changed markedly.

The most shocking feature is the stagnant numbers of coloured Afrikaans-speaking students. This was above all the community SU should have targeted for redress. The intake of black South Africans at SU was not of such a magnitude that it justified English becoming the main medium of instruction.

In the last two years of his term Brink increasingly viewed SU in corporatist terms and rejected the idea that it should be responsive to a particular cultural community. This is revealed in an exchange between Tony Leon, leader of the Democratic Alliance, a liberal opposition party supported in the 1999 election by 80 % of the Afrikaners, and Brink. Leon (pers. comm.) recounts:

Table 6.4: Language Profile of SU Undergraduate Students

	2005	2015
White students		
Afrikaans	8,308	7,285
English	2,461	5,132
Coloured students		
Afrikaans	1,364	1,513
English	613	2,164
Black students		
Afrikaans	18	22
English	325	674
Other	195	1,337
Total	13,284	18,127

Source: SU Data

> When in around 2004 I [...] made the unremarkable observation that there should be two Afrikaans universities in SA, one in the North and the other, obviously, in Stellenbosch, situated in a province with an Afrikaans majority, Brink wrote me a furious response essentially telling me (then the leader of a party which the clear majority of Afrikaners supported) to mind my own business and accused me of interfering with SU's academic freedom![10]

It was almost as if Brink saw himself as SU's managing director overseeing a business in which the student fees and the subsidies generated by its researchers gave the university the right to decide how to conduct its business. Behind this lay the assumption that a government keen on anglicizing the HAUs would back him up. The electoral system of proportional representation on a closed list made local pressure impossible.

In 2016 the SU management published a draft new language policy in terms of which all lectures had to be given in English, while Afrikaans could also be used in strictly circumscribed cases. SU asked interested parties to comment on it. In its submission the executive committee of the Convocation of Alumni rejected this proposal and submitted its own language policy which made Afrikaans the main medium of instruction. A member of the committee sent its proposal to J.M. Coetzee, winner of the Nobel Prize for literature in 2003, and asked his response. Coetzee replied:

> My sympathies are all on your side. The crucial fact, for me is that the official 'Taalbeleid' [language policy] document does not once use the word 'kultuur'. The university management seems to conceive of language as an instrumental communication system without any culture bearing role. (Giliomee 2019, p. 321)

In another submission, the Federation of Governing Bodies of South African Schools, to which the school boards of most Afrikaans schools are affiliated, asked SU not to diminish the use of Afrikaans as a medium in any way (Fedsas 2016).

SU's management ignored these submissions. In 2017 it announced its new policy in which it commits itself to provide all instruction in English. Afrikaans would only be used if the majority of students in a course requested it and if a lecturer able to teach in Afrikaans was available.

The Betrayal of Pledges

The scaling down of Afrikaans at the HAUs is a tale of deceit and duplicity. Those pushing for English to replace Afrikaans knew all too well that a major public controversy would erupt if they spelled out their intentions openly and defended their actions publicly. They preferred to do it by stealth. Barnard Beukman (2016), editor of the Afrikaans daily *Beeld*, formulates it well when he states that at the UFS, UP and SU the process of changing the language of instruction is a tale of "flagrant breaches of public promises, coat turning and double talk."

The courts were so openly biased against Afrikaans that it severely damaged faith in the Constitution among minorities. As mentioned above, in the case of UFS, the Contitutional Court accepted the management's unsubstantiated argument that parallel-medium amounted to segregation. The Chief Justice, who wrote the judgement, even refused a suggestion by one of the dissenting judges that the matter be referrred to the Appeals Court, which could instruct the university to provide evidence.

The UP committed itself in 2010 to retain Afrikaans as a medium of instruction in certain core modules only to abolish Afrikaans-medium instruction six years later. Grové pointed out that parents sent their children to Afrikaans-medium schools anticipating that they would be able to study in Afrikaans at a university. He asked: "Will the UP in future be regarded as an institution that cannot be trusted with regard to any assurances that it gives?" (2016, p. 5–6).

In the Western Cape the movement *Gelyke Kanse*/Equal Opportunities took SU to the Cape High Court for violating its own language policy of 2014, which made provision for instruction in both English and Afrikaans on undergraduate level. In the court proceedings SU admitted that a fifth of its lecturers could not teach in Afrikaans and that the university violated its own language policy in the case of 268 modules. In the case of UP and SU the university management caved in after a group of militant students protested against the Afrikaans offer.

Danie Goosen, chairperson of a federation of Afrikaans cultural associations, issued a public statement in which he denounced the management's going back on its words. He stated: "They broke solemn promises and deliberately misled the public. University managements should not be dismayed if they in future are treated with the greatest possible contempt" (Goosen 2016, translated from Afrikaans).

With Potchefstroom left as the only campus offering an undergraduate degree in Afrikaans, the *Solidariteit* movement, which has both a trade union and a cultural arm, has introduced distance learning by way of modern technology. It has founded Akademia, an Afrikaans-medium tertiary education institution based on the Christian faith and community values. It has so far established thirteen study centers across the country (and one in Windhoek), each of which is equipped with modern conference technology. Each center offers free internet access to an online support system and library. At present Akademia offers four B.Com degrees and a B. Social Sciences degree (Politics, Philosophy and Economics).

The burning question is whether Afrikaans-medium high schools are not destined to become English-medium institutions. In 2010, Theo du Plessis (p. 143), head of language management and practice at UFS, mentioned that meetings were being held in which parents deliberated over whether they should continue to put their children in Afrikaans-medium secondary schools. The question is now so much more urgent.

Conclusion

In 2005 Edwin Hertzog as chairman of the SU Council stated that the main reason why SU should not be predominantly Afrikaans was the risk of isolation and academic mediocracy (Giliomee and Schlemmer 2006, p. 112). This is a strange statement, similar to the one made by John X. Merriman just after Unification. By contrast, SU along with the four other HAUs used mother-tongue instruction in a way that enabled their alumni to distinguish themselves nationally and internationally.

Afrikaans-medium instruction fostered among its students and alumni an ethos and a sense of belonging, together with a language and a culture that articulated an intellectual tradition of its own. The well-known African-born intellectual Mahmood Mamdani recently hailed the Afrikaners' success in turning Afrikaans into a university language and developing their own culture and intellectual traditions (cf. above).

In the course of the twentieth century people trained at the HAUs indeed made their mark both in South Africa and abroad. But as a result of apartheid the world increasingly isolated South Africa and the HAUs in particular. International exchanges between universities in South Africa and those other parts of the world have blossomed after the inauguration of a negotiated democratic order in 1994.

Some supporters of the HAUs' switch to English tried to argue that a good command of English is essential in a world in which English is so dominant as *lingua franca*. The fact, however, is that Afrikaans speakers in general are more bilingual today than ever.

Afrikaans-medium instruction has been undermined by efforts of the university management to climb on the international ratings tables, the intake of large numbers of students who demanded instruction in English and the ANC Government, which refused to fund parallel-medium instruction and undermined the cultural rights of minorities.

Having chosen to become a predominantly English-medium institution, Stellenbosch University now rates third in the country behind the University of Cape Town and Witwatersrand University. This is a major achievement if one takes into account that in the early 1980s it was ranked among the lowest in terms of research output. The University of Pretoria has also made great strides in terms of its research output. The HAUs' switch to English has, however, also come at a great cost. Firstly, no progress is possible with respect to the failure rate of coloured Afrikaans speakers at university level, which is the worst of all communities. Secondly, Afrikaans-medium instruction at secondary school level will increasingly come under pressure with English becoming the preferred medium as a preparation for university. Over the longer run, this switch would undermine Afrikaans as a literary and academic language. Finally, the major setbacks Afrikaans has received over the past two decades as a language of instruction at both high school and university level will only strengthen government policy of persisting with English-medium instruction at a far too early stage. This has been one of the most important reasons for a democratic South Africa failing to realize its promise.

Notes

1. I wish to thank Niek Grové, Albert Grundlingh and Flip Smit for their valuable comments. The interpretations and conclusions are my own.
2. See Table 2.8.
3. E-mail communication, 10 March 2019.
4. The figures for 2018 do not add up because they give a figure of 9 512 for a category designated as "unknown". There is no such category in the case of the 1986 or 2014 figures. Most "unknowns" in the 2018 count were probably white students who in principle refused to designate themselves. This would partly explain the drop in the white students figures from 166,172 in the 2014 to 148,802 in 2018.
5. E-mail communication, 3 April 2016.
6. Personal communication from a lecturer who requested anonymity, 26 November 2003.
7. Letter from Piet Marais to Frederik Willem de Klerk from 16 September 1993. This was delivered to the author in a memo and is now lodged in the Stellenbosch University Library Ms Collection.
8. Through personal interview with Jacko Maree, 21 April 1998.
9. Judgement in the Gauteng division of the High Court, 12 December 2016.
10. E-mail communication, 26 December 2016.

References

Address by President Nelson Mandela on the occasion of his acceptance of an honorary doctorate of the University of Stellenbosch, (Stellenbosch University, 1996), < https://www.sun.ac.za/english/Documents/Madiba/Madibaspeech1996.pdf>.

African National Congress, *Negotiations: a Strategic Perspective* (1992).

AfriForum and Another v University of the Free State, ZACC 48, 2017, <http://www.saflii.org/za/cases/ZACC/2017/48.pdf>.

Altbach, Philip, and Ellen Hazelkorn, 'Why Universities Should Quit the Ratings Game', *University World News* 442 (2017), < https://www.universityworldnews.com/post.php?story=20170105122700949>.

Beeld (15 January 2017).

Beeld (8 March 2018a).

Beukman, Barnard, 'Editorial', *Beeld* (23 July 2016).

Botha, Jan, 'Akademiese werk aan die US van 1918 tot 2018', in Albert Grundlingh, ed., *Die Universiteit van Stellenbosch, 1918–2018* (Stellenbosch: Stellenbosch University, 2018).

de Klerk, Frederik Willem, 'Hof versaak minderhede', *Rapport* (21 January 2018).

De Lannoy, Ariane, Sharlene Swartz, L. Lake and C. Smith, eds, *South African Child Gauge 2015* (Cape Town: Children's Institute, University of Cape Town, 2015).

Die Burger (26 October 2005).

Du Plessis, Theodorus, 'Taalbeleid en onderrigtaalmodus aan die Universiteit van die Vrystaat', in F.W. de Klerk Foundation, ed., *'n Studie oor Afrikaans op Universiteitsvlak* (Cape Town: FW de Klerk Foundation, 2010), 120–147.

du Toit, Pierre, 'Dis tyd vir 'n opvolg-schikking', *Die Burger* (1 October 2000).

Fedderke, Johannes W., 'The Objectivity of the National Research Foundation Peer Review in South Africa Assessed Against Bibliometric Indexes, *Scientometrics* 97/2 (2013), 177–206.

Fedsas, 'Kommentaar op voorgestelde US Taalbeleid', Fedsas website (22 April 2016).

Gelyke Kanse, 'Tale en Dekolonisasie', *Beeld* (23 June 2018b).

Giliomee, Hermann, *Historian: An Autobiography* (University of Virginia Press, 2017).

Giliomee, Hermann, *The Rise and Demise of the Afrikaners* (Tafelberg, 2019).

Giliomee, Hermann, and Schlemmer, Lawrence, *`n Vaste Plek vir Afrikaans: Taaluitdagings op Kampus* (SUN Press, 2006).

Giliomee, Hermann, et al., eds, *Kruispad: Die toekoms van Afrikaans as openbare taal* (Tafelberg, 2001).

Goosen, Danie, 'FAK oor Afrikaans as universiteitstaal', *Maroela Media* (23 February 2016), < https://maroelamedia.co.za/debat/meningsvormers/fak-oor-afrikaans-as-universiteitstaal/>.

Gqirana, Thulani, 'Difference between Black and White Students Failure Rate a "Horror"', *News24* (16 November 2016).

Grové, Niek, *Submission to the Transformation Panel of the UP Council* (2016).

Grundlingh, Albert, 'Die US en die veranderende nasionalistiese strominge en taal oor 'n honderd jaar', in Albert Grundlingh, ed., *Die Universiteit van Stellenbosch, 1918–2018* (Stellenbosch: Stellenbosch University, 2018).

Hill, Lloyd, 'The Decline of Academic Bilingualism in South Africa', *Language Policy* 8/4 (2009), 327–349.

Kane-Berman, John, 'Perpetual Punishment of Afrikaners for the Sins of Their Fathers', Politicsweb Blog (14 January 2018).

Kloss, Heinz, *The Unfolding of Afrikaans in a Germanic, African and a World Context* (University of the North, 1977).

Laponce. Jean, *Languages and Territories* (University of Toronto Press, 1987).

Lehohla, Pali, *Census 2011. Census in Brief* (Pretoria: Statistics South Africa, 2012).

Macmillan, William Miller, *My South African Years* (David Philip, 1975).

Ministry for Education, *Language Policy for Higher Education* (Ministry for Education, 2002).

Ponelis, Fritz, 'Afrikaans as a Language of Science', in Herbert Ernst Wiegand, ed., *Sprache und Sprachen in Wissenschaften* (Walter de Gruyter, 1999).

Rapport, Sake-Rapport (28 April 2018).

Schlemmer, Lawrence, *Voorgraadse Studente op die Universiteit van Stellenbosch: 'n Strategiese Meningsopname* (SU Library Manuscripts Collection, 2008).

Stassen, Nicol, 'Goeie syfers spreek boekdele', *Die Burger* (22 October 2016).

Stassen, Nicol, *Groei in die Afrikaanse en Suid-Afrikaanse Boekbedryf* (Manuscript, 2019).

Stellenbosch Student (August 1943).

Steyn, J., 'Afrikaans by OVS', Afriforum (3 March 2016).

Vaughan, Cristopher L., *On the Shoulders of Oldenburgh: A Biographical Study of the Academic Ratings of South Africa* (The National Research Foundation. 2015).

Eric Mijts

Home Languages and Higher Education: Challenges for Inclusive Higher Education Language Policies for Postcolonial Small Island States in the Twenty-first Century

Estimates claim that almost half the world's children have no access to primary education in their home language and even more have no access to higher education in their home language. The languages used in higher education are limiting the emancipation of speakers of less-favoured languages. This problem is especially poignant in postcolonial regions. In the first place, the lack of recognition for the home language leads to a perceived lack of possibilities of these languages, often combined with a glorification of the former colonizer's language. Secondly, the persistent use of the former colonizer's language in primary and secondary education, leads to (very) high failure rates in schools. This results in low numbers of students in universities and a lack of indigenous/local expertise. Thirdly, as the former colonizer's language is the language of instruction, proficiency in this language is taken for granted and the assessment for any other subject is an assessment of the language proficiency as well. In this chapter, we will discuss this difficult position of the home language and claim that the local universities have to play a pivotal role in the development of local expertise, where possible in the home languages of these regions, with a focus on the value of the mother tongue in the emancipation of the people of the region.

Keywords: postcolonial, small island state, home language, language policy, universities, Aruba, Haiti

In this chapter, I will argue that universities and other institutes of higher education in postcolonial small island states are to play a pivotal role in the protection and promotion of the non-colonial home languages of these small island states, not only in order to promote and protect the languages themselves, but also by using, promoting and protecting these languages in order to contribute to inclusive national development and inclusive higher education. First, I will argue that the continued use of the former colonizer's language in these small island states leads to elite closure, as the elite successfully employs official language policies and their own non-formalized language use patterns to limit the access of non-elite groups to political positions and socio-economic advancement (Myers-Scotton 1993), at the expense of the socio-economic mobility of speakers of the pre-colonial or indigenous and non-colonial (creole and other) languages. I will illustrate this process by looking at two examples: the sovereign state Haiti and the subnational semi-autonomous jurisdiction Aruba, both located in the Caribbean as well as countries where the former colonizer's language plays a pivotal role in education, governance and the judiciary despite the fact that it is a foreign language for more than 90 % of the population. Second, I will argue that universities in postcolonial small island states—and in postcolonial states in general—can either play an important role in the maintenance of this elite closure, or in breaking through it, as universities are socio-economic gatekeepers, limiting access to higher education on the basis of linguistic competence. Third and finally, I will argue that the rise of English as the language of globalisation, academic conversation and student and staff mobility, imposes a burden on the capacity of the universities of these small island states at the expense of their capacity to further develop opportunities for the speakers of the non-colonial home languages of these islands as well as for the languages themselves. I will conclude with an appeal to established academic institutions in these regions that teach in (to varying extents) and protect the home languages of the societies in which they have been established, to continue guarding and fulfilling that major task. On the other hand, where and whenever possible, these institutions should support the development of more academic institutions and departments in the region to develop a significant role for the home language of the people of these countries in the design and implementation of education, service to society and research.

Background

The three concepts 'home languages', 'postcolonial' and 'small island states' deserve further clarification. The concept of *home languages* is a container concept for indigenous languages, creole languages, migrant languages as well as colonial heritage languages. Not all home languages have equal status, as in many cases it is the colonial heritage language that has a dominant position in education, governance and the judiciary while not being the home language of the majority of the population. Due to financial and technical restraints, but also due to a lack of understanding of the importance of language for the socio-economic development of the populations of these countries, indigenous languages and creole languages often have a secondary role in these societies or, in some cases, are even formally excluded from use.

The majority of small island states are former colonies, which legitimizes the fact that they are indicated as *postcolonial* states. However much the use of the term postcolonial may be rejected by those that prefer not to linger in the past, postcolonialism is a present-day concept and a concept of the future. The colonial heritage, including state tradition, institutional and governmental mutual interdependency and also in many cases the use of the colonial heritage language are realities of the present. As such, the postcolonial status of both the former colonizer and the formerly colonized is an important factor in understanding processes in these small island states.

The terminology that is commonly used to refer to *small island states* is SIDS, Small Island Developing States. This terminology, coined by the United Nations (UN), is criticized as it departs from the assumption that these states would have a stronger need to develop than other states, and are as such in a stage of being underdeveloped. Therefore, when referring to these states, I prefer to use small island states instead of small island developing states—while being aware that the concepts of 'smallness' as well as 'insularity' are under debate. The small island states as listed by the UN contain 58 members and associated members, geographically spread over the Pacific, Caribbean, Atlantic, Indian Ocean, Mediterranean and South China Sea. Their status ranges from independent nations (e.g. Haiti, Cabo Verde) to subnational semi-sovereign jurisdictions that either form part of an overseas centralized national authority (e.g. Puerto Rico, Guadeloupe) or form part of broader associations (e.g. Aruba, Cayman Islands). Their territories may be insular, archipelagoes (e.g. Vanuatu, Bahamas), shared insular (e.g. Haiti and Dominican Republic) or peninsular or coastal continental (e.g. Singapore, Belize and Suriname). For this contribution, UN membership or association as a SIDS determines whether a state can be considered to be a small island state or not.

Small island states are studied as a separate category of states as their geographic and demographic characteristics constitute challenges for sustainable development (Briguglio 2003) that include challenges for socio-economic development, education and justice. Due to their scale and isolation, the autonomous development and maintenance of contextually situated institutions and policies impose a relatively high burden on the available resources and manpower of these states. In most postcolonial small island states, this leads to the adoption of institutional structures, policies and practices that have been borrowed from the former colonizer, and to a dependency on external consultancy and quality control. This would not be a challenge if the conditions of these states were similar, but that is not the case. Postcolonial power inequality, in combination with differences in scale, isolation, demographic characteristics, norms and values, religious backgrounds or geological and climatological vulnerabilities are some of the differences that determine that the structures, policies and practices that have been adopted from the former colonizer do not fit the postcolonial societies on which they are being imposed.

Language Use in Postcolonial Regions

One of the striking differences between the formerly colonized and the former colonizer is their use of languages in society. The continued use of the former colonizer's language for education, governance and the judiciary in the geographically heterogeneous multilingual small island states leads to exclusive socio-economic development that favours the elite groups and individuals that are proficient in that language, whereas it forms an obstacle to socio-economic development of the majority of the population for whom that language is a foreign language that impairs their access to educational progress, access to governmental and/or judicial services, and part of the labour market on the basis of language requirements/skills (Mijts 2009). As mentioned in the introduction, the continued use of the former colonizer's language in these small island states leads to elite closure, as the elite successfully employ official language policies and their own non-formalized language use patterns to limit access of non-elite groups to political positions and socio-economic advancement (Myers-Scotton 1993), at the expense of the socio-economic mobility of speakers of the pre-colonial (so called indigenous) and non-colonial (creole and other) languages. Language is a powerful tool, and in postcolonial small island states, the use of the former colonizer's language, with its legal, institutional, and academic support from the former colonizer's universities and institutions, in education and in higher education, does not contribute to the emancipation of the peoples of the former colonies, but contributes to the continuation of an exclusive system in which that language functions as a gatekeeper to political, academic and societal power. In countries like the island states Aruba and Curaçao, which used to be part of the former Netherlands Antilles, the majority of the population speaks Papiamento or Papiamentu. However, Dutch—a foreign language for 94 % of the population—has been maintained as an official language, and as the language of instruction in schools, the language of the judiciary and legislation, and it still plays an important role in governance and law enforcement. In Haiti, independent since 1804, French—a foreign language for 95 % of the population—has been maintained as an official language, the language of education and language of governance, legislation and the judiciary (DeGraff 2017). The use of languages in these three countries illustrates the exclusive character of the use of the colonial heritage language: educational success is low (Migge, Léglise and Bartens 2010; DeGraff 2016), trust in governance is low, socio-economic mobility is low and the judicial system uses a language that is a foreign language to the majority of the population. Although not all challenges in education, governance, and the judiciary can be attributed to the use of language (consider other contributing factors such as lack of funding, lack of expertise, lack of infrastructure), it is obvious that the structural use of a foreign language cannot be the ideal medium for successful inclusive education, governance, or judiciary.

I also need to provide some clarity about the perspective on inclusivity that is taken here: when talking about inclusive language policies for higher education and inclusive language policies in general, this contribution aims at a maximisation of inclusivity now, for all speakers of all languages, and not at a future of one homogenized anglophone (and as such anglocentric and anglo-favouring) sphere in which languages other than the *lingua franca* of globalisation, English, have been eroded, suppressed or replaced. This also means the acknowledgement and recognition of the inevitability of multilingual development and the recognition of linguistic rights of speakers of disadvantaged languages. Finally, one has to accept that solutions for inclusive multilingual development require efforts from institutions, governments and individuals in society for mutual understanding and acceptance of linguistic diversity.

Following Phillipson (2013), and expanding his analysis of linguistic imperialism to all languages of colonial powers, one needs to deconstruct the roles of the former colonizers' languages and the underlying belief systems. Phillipson distinguishes the structural infrastructural privileged status, ideological glorification, normality or hegemony of the language and the often subtractive character of the use of that language that leads to exploitation, injustice, inequality, and hierarchy that privileges those able to use the dominant language more than others. Linguistic imperialism, however much contested and resisted, interlocks with a structure of imperialism in culture, education, the media, communication, the economy, politics and military activities (Phillipson 2013). I add to Phillipson's deconstruction the structural legal and governmental embeddedness of the former colonizers' languages, not as legal transplants, but as an uncomfortable heritage from the colonial past (Bröring and Mijts 2018) and as a form of maintenance of the former colonizers' language regimes by means of path dependency and state tradition (Sonntag and Cardinal 2015). Due to processes of elite formation and the privileges of the users of the standard forms of the colonial languages, the emancipation of populations that do not speak the colonial languages is severely limited. The former colonizer's language "was the official vehicle and the magic formula to colonial elitedom" (Ngũgĩ 1985, p. 115). Twentieth and twenty-first century globalisation and the rise of the role of English in the non-English speaking world have added an extra dimension: in the colonial past, the formerly colonized had to master the language of the former colonizer in order to achieve access to socio-economic mobility, now, the formerly colonized need to master both the former colonizer's language *and*

English as a tool for emancipation. This represents, yet again, a continuation of the policies of colonial times (Phillipson 2013; Mohanty 2016; Mijts 2017).

Universities in postcolonial small island states—and in postcolonial states in general—can and should play a pivotal role in the emancipation of the home languages, and by extension of their speakers, other than the colonial heritage language. These universities are gatekeepers to socio-economic development as the use of the former colonizer's language in higher education limits access to higher education on the basis of linguistic competence. However, in many formerly colonized nations, the language of instruction in—part of—the educational system is the former colonizer's language. For example in Haiti, French, a foreign language for 95 % of the population, is maintained as the main language of instruction in secondary and tertiary education, and is still used in many primary schools; in Aruba, Bonaire and Curaçao, Dutch is still widely used as language of instruction in primary, secondary and higher education. Currently, however, more and more postcolonial educational systems develop programmes in the home languages of the people of these countries. DeGraff and Stump claimed in their 2018 publication on Kreyol in Haiti that "local languages, coupled with modern pedagogy and technology, are necessary, though not sufficient, ingredients for universal access to quality education" (DeGraff and Stump 2018). It is not only the language that will create equal opportunity, but language is an indispensable condition for the development of equal opportunity inclusive education in these countries; not using the home languages is a guarantee for the development of an exclusive system that only benefits a small part of society.

For so many people in this world, it is not possible to study in their home language. Estimates claim that almost half the world's children have no access to primary education in their home language and even more have no access to higher education in their home language. "In primary schools across the world, 40 % of students must learn all academic subjects, including how to read, in a language that they do not speak fluently" (UNESCO 2016). Excluding students' native languages from the classroom leads to academic failure for hundreds of millions of children throughout the world (Walter 2008) and contributes to their communities' socio-economic underdevelopment (Philipson 1994, quoted in DeGraff 2018). Faraclas (2016) claims that more than 50 % of students must learn in a language that they do not speak fluently, also pointing out the severe negative influence this can have on the academic development of these children, and by extension, the future socio-economic possibilities these children can have.

Emancipation of languages, and by extension their users, can only be achieved through major shifts in the belief systems of those involved. This process can span generations, not only challenging the policy and practices of the powers that be, but also challenging the traditional values of these communities that have been ingrained with beliefs of linguistic inferiority and inadequateness (Mijts, Faraclas and Kester 2018).

Case 1: Aruba

The case study of multilingualism in Aruba demonstrates that linguistic inequality can be codified in law, and can actually, in spite of convincing evidence of the inadequateness of the use of the former colonizer's language in several domains, be maintained. Aruba is a small island state of less than 180 square kilometers in the Caribbean where four languages are dominant in different domains of language use. A majority of the Aruban-born population speaks all four dominant languages: Papiamento, Dutch, English and Spanish. All four languages can be considered to be dominant languages: Papiamento is an official language and the home language of 68 % of the population of the island; Dutch—spoken by 6 % of the population—is the other official language and the dominant language of the Kingdom of the Netherlands to which Aruba belongs; English—spoken as a home language by 8 %—is the dominant language of tourism, the predominant industry in Aruba; and Spanish—spoken as home language by 14 %—is the language of nearby Venezuela and Colombia, and as such it is the regionally dominant language (Mijts and Waterman 2017).

In Aruba, just like in many other postcolonial states, time and again, critical junctures have not led to decisions that favour the mother tongue of the majority of the population over Dutch (Winkel 1955; Prins-Winkel 1973; Dijkhoff and Pereira 2010; Mijts 2014). Before 2003, Dutch was the only official language in Aruba, since 2003, both Dutch and Papiamento have official status. In many publications, this status of Papiamento is uncritically acclaimed as Papiamento having the same legal status as Dutch and as such having full legal recognition. Unfortunately, this is not the case.

Language legislation, and legislation in general, in Aruba represents the uneasy postcolonial relations with the Kingdom of the Netherlands. The main legislation that prescribes or describes language use in Aruba are the Official Languages Ordinance (2003) and the Primary Education Ordinance (1989). This Aruban legislation on languages positions Papiamento as a language that is at best tolerated and at worst excluded from use. The Official Languages Ordinance, article 2, states that Papiamento and Dutch are the official languages of Aruba. In this article, contrary to alphabetical order, Papiamento precedes Dutch in an apparent symbolic attempt to put emphasis on the role of Papiamento in Aruban society. Article 3 of the same ordinance regulates the use of languages in interaction between citizens and government. It does give both parties the authority to communicate in one of the two official languages, but it does not provide a guarantee to the citizens that the government will use the language of the citizen. Both citizen and government are free to use the language of their choosing. The law makes provision for translation, but only at the expense of the citizen who requests it, and without any guarantee of quality.

Articles 4.1 and 4.2, which regulate languages used in an oath, promise or statement, present Papiamento as an accepted alternative for Dutch. The phrasing "instead of the legally prescribed Dutch words, one is allowed to use the corresponding Papiamento words" does not give both languages equal status, but instead positions Dutch as the norm and Papiamento as an acceptable alternative.

Article 5 contains only five words, but these words are crucial: "Wetgeving geschiedt in het Nederlands" ("The language of legislation is Dutch"). In this article, the language of legislation is prescribed; no provisions have been made in this law that stipulate how the government might provide translations of legislation in the people's language. Ignorance of the law excuses no one, but how are you supposed to know the law if the law does not speak your language? Further stressing the exclusive use of Dutch in legal matters, article 6 states that the language of criminal proceedings is Dutch. Even though there are minimum requirements laid down in international law on the availability of court interpreters, this practice in which the judicial process is organized around the linguistic skills of the judicial system and not of the population is questionable. The fact that no formal training for Papiamento—Dutch translators and interpreters is available further problematizes this situation.

Education in the multilingual state of Aruba poses its challenges. Educational success is low, dropout ratios are high and the failure rate of those who make it to higher education is high as well. This results in a low percentage of higher educated Aruban citizens in society and on the labour market. Multiple reports and publications over more than five decades attribute this low success rate mainly to the choice of the Dutch language as medium of instruction in primary education. The use of Dutch, or an artificial form of Dutch, given that most pupils and teachers are Papiamento-speaking, alienates pupils from the educational process and creates extra obstacles to academic success. Still, this practice is prescribed by law. The Ordinance for Primary Education treats Dutch as the norm: article 9 prescribes Dutch as the official language of education, except for the first two years of kindergarten. Only recently, a special ruling by the Minister of Education has allowed Papiamento to be used as the language of instruction.

Aruban law stipulates that the language of the former colonizer is to be preferred over the language of the majority of the population.

A last example concerns the Dutch nationality law and thus takes us beyond the borders of the country of Aruba up to the level of legislation of the Kingdom of the Netherlands that applies to four countries: Aruba, Curaçao, the Netherlands and Sint Maarten. It is interesting to note that during the discussions on this law in the Aruban national Parliament, this legislation was presented as a symbolic recognition of the importance of the Papiamento language. Article 8d of this law stipulates the linguistic requirements for the acquisition of state citizenship: if one wants to become a national of the Kingdom of the Netherlands, while resident and complying with all other requirements, one must submit proof of sufficient knowledge of the Dutch language. Yet, residents applying for the same citizenship in Aruba, Curaçao, Sint Maarten and the Netherlands Caribbean island municipalities of Bonaire, Sint Eustatius and Saba, must submit proof of knowledge of the Dutch language *as well as* the prevailing language of that territory. Unfortunately, this condition limits the possibilities for these islands to integrate residents who want to become citizens, because they must pass two language tests instead of one. Moreover, one of these language tests poses particular problems for most potential candidates, since Dutch is not present in the media, in the linguistic landscape or on the labour market of these islands. The double language test that was hailed as a recognition of the islands' languages in fact has become an extra obstacle, potentially limiting the full social and legal integration of long term residents of these islands.

This brief analysis demonstrates that, despite the fact that former colonial ties have been replaced by a different set of relations designed ostensibly to take the Kingdom of the Netherlands into the twenty-first century, the laws concerning language on Aruba are a paradigmatic example of how the state traditions of the Netherlands continues in the legislation of the now officially autonomous islands of the Kingdom, in spite of solid evidence that the language policy that results from this legislation does not appear to lead to favourable results for the populations of the islands. The voice of the people of the nation of Aruba that should be represented in law appears to be overruled by voices that represent the former colonizer's truths and state traditions. The continuing predominance of the metropolitan state tradition which has always favoured the Dutch language is demonstrated in the formulation of legislation in which the mother tongues of the overwhelming majority of the populations of the islands are at best presented as an acceptable alternative to Dutch, and at worst excluded from use in key areas where citizens' rights are at play: in education, the judiciary, law-making, and even in the people's right to citizenship.

Despite the presumed equality for Papiamento and Dutch in the Official Languages Ordinance, Aruban law confirms the dominant position of Dutch over Papiamento as a continuation of European Dutch state tradition in government, education and law/legal practice. The 2019 National Education Policy of the ministry of Education, Science and Sustainable Development of Aruba stipulates the introduction of the *Skol Multilingual* in all Aruban primary schools, an educational model that focuses on the development of academic skills using Papiamento, the language of the majority of the children as well as the teachers in the Aruban schools, as the language of instruction. The reception of this change demonstrates how deeply rooted the belief is that success can only be achieved through the former colonizer's language, Dutch. However, if the implementation of the plan can get sufficient support and is successful, this action could be a great example for other countries that are struggling with similar challenges.

Case 2: Haiti

The second case study focuses on the position of French and Kreyòl in Haiti, in order to demonstrate that the adoption of the former colonizer's governmental, legal and educational structures leads to legal frameworks and policy constructions that do not benefit the majority of the citizens of the islands, but are geared towards conformity with the former colonizer's frameworks on the basis of a perceived or constructed benefit for the people of the small island states involved. The example of Aruba has sufficiently demonstrated that in recent decolonisation processes, the home languages of the majority of the population can be neglected, whereas the former colonizer's language is given a pivotal position in postcolonial societies. A small-scale study of the development of language policies and practices in Haiti demonstrates that even in a country where colonisation has ended more than 200 years ago, the adoption of the language of the former colonizer prevails over the adoption of the language(s) of the people of the country in legislation, the judiciary and in educational practice. In Haiti, as in so many postcolonial states, the recognition of the home language of the people is a long and painful process that fails to recognize the needs of the people of that country.

The Republic of Haiti, the country that forms the western half of Hispaniola, is home to about 11 million inhabitants. Despite the huge differences in population and size, it shares multiple common characteristics with Vanuatu and Aruba; it shares the adoption of the former colonizer's language as a common trait. 95 % of the country reports to speak Kreyòl as their home language, only 5 % reports to be francophone. However, up until now, nearly the whole structure of the education system in Haiti, along with its language policies and instructional practices, is evocative of the colonial past of the country (Marky 2016, p. 13). The Haitian revolution (1791–1804) led to the establishment of the sovereign state of Haiti in 1804, the first independent nation of the Caribbean as the outcome of the slave revolt. The Constitution of 1805 was drafted in French, just like all subsequent Constitutions. From the onset of the nation, the establishment of schools throughout the country has been a point of great attention in legislation. Nevertheless, until today, access to education and educational materials remains a matter of social class and the different values attributed to French and Kreyòl remain a serious problem (Marky 2016). The first constitutional stipulation on the use of languages was in article 24 of the Constitution of 1918, in which French was declared to be the official language, and its use was made mandatory in administrative and judiciary matters. The Constitution of 1964 was the first to mention Kreyòl as it made an allowance for the use of the language to safeguard the material and moral interests of those who had insufficient knowledge of French (article 35). The Constitution of 1983 maintained French as the official language, but also stipulated that French and Kreyòl are the national languages (article 62). This constitutional position of French as the sole official language of the country was maintained until 1987.

The use of French in legislation and the judiciary has led to international critique for Haiti. In 1979, the Inter-American Committee for Human Rights concluded that in Haiti

> Many of the accused persons held in Port-au-Prince (and of course in other urban areas) are poor and illiterate, hardly speak or understand French (which is the official language of the Court), and have a very poor understanding of how Haitian justice works. Moreover, despite the government's efforts in this regard, the Haitian people are not always fully aware of the rights guaranteed to all citizens by the Penal Code and the Constitution of Haiti. (OAS 1979)

Up until today, French is the language in which legal proceedings are conducted and legal materials are printed (UPR Working Group 2016). It was not until 1987 that the Haitian Constitution recognized Kreyòl as the common unifying language and included Kreyòl as an official language, alongside French. Article 5 states that "all Haitians are united by a common language: Creole. Creole and French are the official languages of the Republic". It may be considered a symbolic choice to put Kreyòl first (article 62 of the Constitution of 1983 still put French first, in spite of the alphabetical order), in recognition of the value of the language for the population of Haiti.

Article 40 of that same Constitution regulates the government's duty to provide information in both languages:

> The State has the obligation to publicize in the oral, written and televised press in the Creole and French languages all laws, orders, decrees, international agreements, treaties, and conventions on everything affecting the national life, except for information concerning national security.

There is even the constitutional guarantee that "a Haitian Academy shall be established to standardize the Creole language and enable it to develop scientifically and harmoniously" (article 213). In retrospect, it is painful to observe that this constitution that finally recognizes Kreyòl was published in French, and that no official translation of this constitution in Kreyòl became available. The establishment of the Haitian academy had to wait for a long time: it took until 2015 to establish the *Akademi Kreyòl Ayisyen*, 28 years after the constitution mandated its establishment.

The dominance of the French language in education is recognized as a fundamental issue for the development of an inclusive Haitian society and the use of French in education in Haiti is deemed to be the core of the failure of Haitian education (Dejean 2010; Hebblethwaite 2012; DeGraff 2016). Despite the fact that French is not the home language of the majority of both the teachers and the students in schools, and despite the fact that educational attainment in Haiti is extremely low, French is still maintained as the language of instruction and is still seen as the—only—gateway to educational success (Avalos and Augustin 2018).

The constitutional—mainly symbolic—protection of Kreyòl does not provide sufficient guarantees for the Haitian population. The maintained adoption of French, and not of the language of the majority of the people of Haiti in education, government and the judiciary excludes the vast majority of the population from equal opportunities in all three terrains. Even after more than 200 years of sovereignty, the Haitian state has failed to shake off the former colonizer's language, and maintains that language, as well as the related institutional structures and practices at the expense of its own people's development.

The tension between legislation, practice and attitudes demonstrates that despite processes of decolonisation, one cannot make the claim that decolonisation is completed—or can ever be completed. Law alone will not solve the postcolonial challenges for the population. A change in attitude—or an increased linguistic awareness—may lead to counter-hegemonic action, action that deserves support from institutions, including the universities of these societies. These universities have a hard time fulfilling that role as they are torn between a drive for academic recognition by the academic institutions of the former colonizer, the limited resources that they have at their disposal, political influence and often ignorance about the role universities can play in society.

Language Perception and the Role of Institutions

In the first place, the lack of recognition and the ensuing lack of status of the home languages of these peoples lead to a perceived lack of possibilities of use of these languages, often combined with a glorification of the former colonizer's language. To provide an example: in recent social media discussions on language in Aruba, an argument that is often heard in the discussion on the language of instruction in schools is that Papiamento is a minority language. However, Dutch is the fourth language of the island in numbers after Papiamento, Spanish and English, and still that language—Dutch—is, by law, the language of instruction in schools. In these same conversations, Papiamento is said to be an incomplete or imperfect language, not fit for academic purposes, but is this something we can say about any language? There is no such thing as a standard for academic suitability of a language. Putting down Papiamento as a language that is unfit for academic use resembles the statements about Dutch in the discussions on the introduction of Dutch in higher education in Leuven. This was even underscored by Cardinal Mercier in his infamous letter of instructions in 1906 about Dutch as a language for higher education: French was supposed to be superior and more adequate for the expression of complex thought patterns. Cardinal Mercier is very well-respected for his work in other fields, but in this case, history has proven him wrong, and will keep on proving these kinds of statements wrong as the use of a language in academic settings will automatically induce the further development of that language. Apart from that, would it not be the home language of the people of a certain region that is most adequate to describe the challenges faced by the people of that region? And consequentially, would it not be the language that is most adequate for discussing these challenges with the peoples of these regions?

Secondly, the persistent use of the former colonizer's languages in primary and secondary education leads to low participation levels and high failure rates in schools. This results in low numbers of students in universities and a lack of indigenous/local expertise, which in turn leads to an elite status for those that do succeed.

Thirdly, as the former colonizer's language is the language of instruction, proficiency in this language is taken for granted and students in schools and universities are corrected as if they are mother tongue speakers of that language. Their assessment for any other subject, ranging from mathematics to geography to history, is an assessment of their language proficiency as well. For a local teacher within this system, this leads to an absurd double bind in which that teacher will teach pupils sharing the same L1 as her or him in a foreign language.

The rise of English as the language of globalisation, academic conversation and student and staff mobility, imposes a burden on the capacity of the universities of these small island states at the expense of their capacity to further develop opportunities for the speakers of the home languages of these islands and the languages themselves. Erasmus+ and other internationalisation efforts create great opportunities for the development of international networks, the development of intercultural understanding, the exchange of knowledge and much more. However, internationalisation and globalisation also pose a threat.

Let's first look at the bright side. The Erasmus programme actually claims to aim at linguistic diversity and language learning—this was ingrained in the original set up of the programme—but in practice, the outcome is the opposite: the programme has given rise to a globalizing English *lingua franca* among the Erasmus travelers, and little language learning. The larger European non-anglophone universities ring the alarm bell on the pressure of globalisation and the threat to the use and study of the home languages and national languages as well as the threat this would pose to the quality of education.

The—usually smaller—institutes of higher education in small island states are less equipped to deal with this pressure. The language policies of these institutions cannot deal with the pressures of internationalisation and the consequences for the use and study of languages in their programmes adequately. The past decade has shown programmes in higher education in these island states to shift to English, whereas promotion and inclusive practice accommodating the people of the societies in and for whom these universities have been set up, does not become a reality. The efforts invested in the development of English-language-of-instruction programmes in these states are at the detriment of the capacity for the development of initiatives that favour the home languages of these territories. Incentives for teaching of and in other home languages are scarce, nor are there any incentives for publications in Papiamento or for research lines in any of the domains and fields mentioned above. As time and finances are scarce, the development of materials, programmes and curricula is mainly dependent on the efforts of a small group of pioneers. There is—in general—no institutional recognition for, nor promotion of, academic production in home languages and there is a lack of language policies—at all.

The use of foreign languages in education leads to linguistic inequality: an educational system that is based on the former colonizer's language and that adopts the language of globalisation is per definition not inclusive for the speakers of the other home languages that are the demographically dominant languages in that area. An often underestimated consequence is the silencing of the peoples of these communities, and their lack of participation in the academic debate. The peoples of these island states have often been overcorrected by native speakers of the former colonizer's languages. This has led to a strong reluctance of public speaking and writing. This lack of participation in the academic debate also leads to an alienation from what the academic world has to offer. Non-inclusive higher education creates socio-economic inequality and, as a consequence, dependency on external expertise and consultancy, brain drain and financial losses for these states as well. Does attention for the home language mean that you do not want to participate in the international academic debate? Who says so and why? Should this not be turned around: is it so that if you want to participate in the international academic debate, you are excused from—or even forbidden to—participate in the national debate? The answer is simple: no! But, we have not yet created tools that stimulate the production and dissemination of academic materials in home languages like Papiamento and Kreyól.

Of course there are examples of universities and other institutes of higher education that do include the study and use of the non-colonial home languages of these islands: take for instance the work of the Jamaican Languages Unit at the University of the West Indies at Mona, the Creole studies programme at the University of the West Indies at Cave Hill, Les Etudes de Kreyòl at Université d'Etat d'Haïti, the professional bachelor's and master's programmes for teachers of Papiamentu at the University of Curaçao, the bachelor's programmes for teachers of Papiamento at Instituto Pedagogico Arubano as well as the increasing inclusion of Papiamento programmes in curricula at the University of Aruba: these are examples of significant steps that are being taken, but more can and should be done.

Academic institutions in the former colonizer's sphere play an important role in education in and protection of the home languages of the societies in which they have been established. They should continue guarding and fulfilling that major task, and on the other hand, where possible, support the development of more academic institutions and departments in those regions where the home language of the people can play a significant role in the design and implementation of education and research.

Conclusion

Emancipation of populations and empowering people is giving them a voice. A voice that is as strong as it can be, not only through the language of the *other*, but through the language of the *self*, their own home language, with respect for the home language and with love for the home language as part of the core of personality and identity.

Make no mistake: I am not saying that all teaching and research at universities in small island states should be primarily focused on research, development and teaching of the home languages; I am not saying that we should ban English or the other world languages (in the case of Aruba that is—interestingly enough—Dutch); nor am I saying that we should turn away from internationalisation and Erasmus+. The issue at hand is not that binary. What I am saying though, is that the—usually—small universities of postcolonial small island states should promote the study and use of the home languages of these regions and should be the front runners in the debates on accessibility of education, the judiciary and governance in the home languages of the people of these states. Some have already taken up this role, but all should. In that path to emancipation of the home languages of these regions and the speakers of these languages, these universities need strong partners in the development of such programmes, partners that also really understand the value of the mother tongue in the emancipation of the people of that region. These partners could and should include the universities and related institutions of the former colonizers, and the partnerships that need to be forged should not be geared towards the promotion of the former colonizer's language, but towards the support of the development and understanding of the position of all languages in these societies.

References

Avalos, Mary, and Jennifer Augustin, 'Haiti's Language-in-Education Policy: Conflicting Discourses at the Local Level' in Ali Fuad Selv and Nathanael Rudolph, eds, *Conceptual Shifts and Contextualized Practices in Education for Glocal Interaction. Intercultural Communication and Language Education* (Singapore: Springer, 2018), 37–54.

Briguglio, Lino, *The Vulnerability Index and Small Island Developing States: A Review of Conceptual and Methodological Issues* (University of Malta, 2003).

Bröring, Herman E., and Eric Mijts, 'Language Planning and Policy, Law and (Post)Colonial Relations in Small Island States: A Case Study', *Social Inclusion*, 5/4 (2017), 29–37.

DeGraff, Michel, 'What Is Education For?', Boston Review (2016), <http://bostonreview.net/forum/what-education/michel-degraff-michel-degraff-responds-danielle-allen>.

DeGraff, Michel, 'La langue maternelle comme fondament du savoir: L'Intiative MIT-Haiti: vers une éducation en créole efficace et inclusive', *Revue transatlantique d'études Suisses* 6/7 (2017), 177–197.

DeGraff, Michel, 'Linguistics' Role in the Right to Education', *Science* 360/6388 (2018), 502.

DeGraff, Michel, and Glenda Stump (2018). 'Kreyòl, Pedagogy, and Technology for Opening Up Quality Education in Haiti: Changes in Teachers' Metalinguistic Attitudes as First Steps in a Paradigm Shift', *Language: Journal of the linguistic society of America* 94/2 (2018), 127–157.

Dejean, Yves, 'Creole and Education in Haiti', in Arthur Spears K. and Carole M. Berotte Joseph, eds, *The Haitian Creole Language: History, Structure, Use, and Education* (Lanham: Lexington Books, 2010), 199–216.

Dijkhoff, Maria, and Joyce Pereira, 'Language and Education in Aruba, Bonaire and Curacao', in Bettina Migge, Isabella Léglise, and Angela Bartens, eds, *Creoles in Education* (Amsterdam: John Benjamins B.V., 2010), 237–272.

Faraclas, Nicholas, Ellen-Petra Kester, Eric Mijts, Santiago Ruiz, and Joel Simo, 'Mother Tongue Literacy in the Caribbean, Latin America and the South Pacific: Community Based Approaches That Promote the Survival of Endangered Languages', in Nicholas Ostler and Panchanan Mohanty, eds, *Language colonization and endangerment: Long- term effects, echoes and reactions* (Hyderabad: University of Hyderabad and Centre for Endangered Languages and Mother Tongue Studies, 2016), 170–175.

Hebblethwaite, Benjamin, 'French and Underdevelopment, Haitian Creole and Development: Educational Language Policy Problems and Solutions in Haiti', *Journal of Pidgin and Creole languages* 27/2 (2012), 255–302.

Marky, Jean-Pierre, *Language and Learning in a Post-colonial Context: A Critical Ethnographic Study in Schools in Haiti* (Florence: Taylor and Francis, 2016).

Migge, Bettina, Isabella Léglise, and Angela Bartens, eds, *Creoles in Education* (Amsterdam: John Benjamins B.V., 2010).

Mijts, Eric, 'Taaleisen in personeelsadvertenties in de Arubaanse kranten', 6de *ANELA Conferentie* (2009), 246–252.

Mijts, Eric, 'Recentering the Focus in Discourse on Education in Postcolonial Small Island States: The Case of Aruba', in Nicholas Faraclas et al., eds, *Creole Connections* (SanJuan/Willemstad: UoC/UPR, 2014), 121–128.

Mijts, Eric, 'State Traditions and Language Regimes in Aruba and Other Small Island States: Some Preliminary Thoughts on the Study of Language Legislation as Discourse', in Nicholas Faraclas et al., eds, *Archaeologies of Erasures and Silences: Recovering Othered Languages, Literatures and Cultures in the Dutch Caribbean and Beyond* (San Juan/Willemstad: University of Puerto Rico/University of Curaçao, 2017), 161–165.

Mijts, Eric, 'In de verdrukking tussen dekolonisatie en globalisering. Thuistalen en hoger onderwijs in kleine eilandstaten' *Ons Erfdeel*, 2018/4 (2018), 178–181.

Mijts, Eric, Nicholas Faraclas, and Ellen-Petra Kester, 'Multilingualism and Education in the Caribbean Netherlands, a Linguist's Contribution to the Development of Sustainable Educational Policy Development in Caribbean Schools. The Case Study of Statia', in Ellen-Rose Kambel, ed., *Multilingualism in the Netherlands* (The Hague: Rutu Foundation, 2018), 107–123.

Mijts, Eric, and Karlijn Waterman, 'Wat is de positie van het Nederlands in de multilinguale samenleving?', in Liesbeth Echteld, Eric Mijts, and Wim Rutgers, eds, *Taalbeleid in het Caribisch Gebied; heden en nabije toekomst, Derde CARAN-conferentie in Curaçao, 16, 17 en 18 november 2015* (Curacao: University of Curacao, 2017), 125– 131.

Ministerie van Onderwijs, Wetenschap en Duurzame Ontwikkeling, *Nationaal Onderwijs Plan* (Aruba: Ministerie van Onderwijs, Wetenschap en Duurzame Ontwikkeling, 2019).

OAS, *Report on the situation of human rights in Haiti* (Inter-American Commission on Human Rights of the Organization of American States, 1979).

Prins-Winkel, Anna Cornelia, *Kabes duru? Verslag van een onderzoek naar de onderwijssituatie op de Benedenwindse eilanden van de Nederlandse Antillen, in verband met het probleem van de vreemde voertaal bij het onderwijs* (Assen: Van Gorcum, 1973).

Mohanty, Ajit, 'Multilingualism and Predicaments of Education in India', in Ofelia Garcia, Tove Skutnabb-Kangas, and Maria. E. Torres-Guzmán, eds, *Imagining Multilingual Schools. Languages in Education and Glocalization* (Clevedon: Multilingual Matters, 2006), 262–283.

Myers-Scotton, Carol, *Social Motivations for Codeswitching. Evidence from Africa* (Oxford: Clarendon, 1993).

Ngũgĩ wa Thiong'o, 'The Language of African Literature', *New Left Review* (1985), 109–127.

Pérez-Milans, Miguel, and James Tollefson, 'Language Policy and Planning: Directions for Future Research' in James Tollefson and Miguel Pérez-Milans, eds, *The Oxford handbook of language policy and planning* (New York: Oxford University Press, 2018), 727–741.

Phillipson, Robert, 'Linguistic Imperialism' in Carol Chapelle, ed., *The Encyclopedia of Applied Linguistics* (Oxford: Blackwell/Wiley, 2013).

Phillipson, Robert, Mart Rannut, and Tove Skutnabb Kangas, eds, *Linguistic Human Rights: Overcoming Linguistic Discrimination* (Berlin/Boston: De Gruyter Mouton, 1994).

Sonntag, Selma K., and Linda Cardinal, 'Introduction: State Traditions and Language Regimes: Conceptualizing Language Policy Choices' in Linda

Cardinal and Selma K. Sonntag, eds, *State traditions and language regimes* (Montreal/Kingston: McGill- Queen's University Press, 2015), 3–26.

UPR Working Group, *Republic of Haiti: Access to judicial remedies in Haiti* (Submission to the United Nations Human Rights Council, 2016).

UNESCO, *If you don't understand, how can you learn? Global Education Monitoring Report* (Policy Paper 24, 2016), <http://unesdoc.unesco.org/images/0024/002437/243713E.pdf>.

Walter, Stephen, 'The Language of Instruction Issue: Framing an Empirical Perspective', in Bernard Spolsky and Francis Hult, eds, *The Handbook of Educational Linguistics* (Malden/Oxford: Blackwell Publishing, 2008), 129–146.

Winkel, Nelly, 'Het taalprobleem in het Antilliaans onderwijs', *Christoffel* 1–2 (1955), 68–78.

Conclusion

Danny Pieters

Policy Suggestions

This conclusion summarizes different ways in which the current wave of internationalisation of universities and the corresponding increase in the use of English holds certain threats for higher education institutions. These threats are coupled to some policy suggestions that can serve as a starting point in the search for a new balance in language policies between internationalisation and the protection of the national language(s).

Keywords: language policy, internationalisation, universities, protection, national language, policy suggestions

Throughout the contributions in this volume, the complex situation of language use in universities has become clear. At first glance, it may sometimes seem that there is a tense relationship between internationalisation and the protection of the national language and culture. Doing one seems to preclude the other. We must not be blinded by this seeming opposition and the prejudices that go hand in hand with it, as some contributions have already shown. This conclusion gives a summary of the (linguistic) challenges that universities face, but also offers a first step towards a policy that remedies these challenges.

Today, you can hear the echo of the opposition between social and national in the discussions concerning the relation between internationalisation and the protection of the own language. Internationalisation, then, is the progressive, forward-looking approach, while protection of the own language is the backward-looking conservative reaction. Such a presentation of facts can be strongly opposed, because this opposition is not necessarily a reality: we should combine our care for the own language and culture with internationalisation. If we are successful in doing so, both will even strengthen each other. Moreover, internationalisation is not progressive or social in itself, while protection of the own language and culture is not necessarily conservative. When internationalisation, often synonymous with the widespread use of English, leads to better communication between academics and students of various countries, it certainly is positive. However, if it leads to the negation of diversity, if it imposes a uniform way of speaking and thus of thinking, we should not be happy with it. This very limited form of internationalisation is paired with a certain (economic) worldview that might even be a threat to universities in their three core tasks: education, research, and service to the communities. In the remainder of this conclusion, this point will be elaborated upon, along with suggestions to work towards genuine internationalisation.

Universities Under Pressure

Universities are under threat in their core tasks for several reasons. First of all, they are confronted with certain demands to emphasize the direct utility of what students are to be taught, prioritizing such over their general development as persons and citizens. Direct utility to the world sounds nice, but it is seldom directed towards service to the poor and the less-developed countries. Direct utility to the world most often means service to the 'established' powers, the big international firms, the world of money.

Universities are also threatened as research is made more and more dependent upon external financing by international actors, some of them non-profit, many pro-profit. The fact that research supports economic development is not wrong at all, but research should not be restricted to doing so. Other values should also play a role in determining research priorities, some of them indeed not linked to the international markets, but to the needs of defined groups of people and communities living in a specific, national context. If we look at certain important non-profit funding institutions, such as the Commission of the European Union, we see that they very much focus on economic return of the research. The European Union may have as its motto 'unity in diversity'; the reality is that outside any international agreement, it *de facto* imposes that all research applications and in fact all research are to be carried out in English. This fits perfectly into their nearly exclusive free market orientation.

Of course science is not linked to a nation or a language. Science by its essence is international. There is no French mathematics, there is only mathematics; there is no German engineering science, there is engineering science. So it is only normal that there is a constant exchange of knowledge and ideas between scientists of all parts of the world. English being the *lingua franca* of the day, this exchange takes place in English. What we should avoid, however, is that the scientific reflection itself is confined to English, that we cannot but use English when we deal with a given academic subject, as that would narrow too much our creativity, our freedom of thinking on the subject. What we cannot accept is that English would inhibit the development of the national language in a whole area of science. In the end, this would make the national language only suited for home, garden and kitchen.

Internationalisation is essential to the development of any science, to research and academic education. The benefits of internationalisation are well described, and the process is seen as evident, being beneficial to both research and education, to both students and professors. Internationalisation should however not necessarily and always mean anglification. It should also leave room for a diversity of important and less important other languages, as this will contribute to a genuine internationalisation rather than oppose it.

Today, internationalisation puts a huge amount of pressure on universities and scientists to use English in academic research, for education, and in administrative contacts with (mainly exchange) students and incoming staff from abroad. Knowledge production typically takes place in international journals that use English. The question is whether this equation between internationalisation and exclusive anglification is appropriate. An open-minded internationalisation requires a variety of languages, one of them—probably for the moment the most important one—being English. Genuine internationalisation does not exclude the use of national and other languages in academic education and research, but rather stimulates it. Genuine internationalisation of academic education and scientific research is well aware of the third, equally important task of the university: service to the community. And let us be clear: service to the community is not the same as providing the businesses of the country with innovative solutions and new market opportunities.

If a university is to realize its triple goal—excellent academic education, outstanding research and service to the community—it has to internationalize while at the same time caring for the language or languages of the communities it serves. Doing both will strengthen both. We can take KU Leuven as an example. The student revolt half a century ago claimed democratisation and the use of the students' own language. It did not lead to a weak, provincial university, but to an internationally-oriented university, servicing the Flemish population and the world with excellent research and education. A university that is internationally oriented, but starts from a strong connection to the community's language and culture in order to be firmly rooted in the community and provide openness for all. How do we get there?

Policy Suggestions

In the second part of this conclusion, we will look into suggestions in order to bring forward the idea of a simultaneous effort of internationalisation and of further protection of the own language and of the linguistic diversity. These suggestions will be made in general terms, but are of course easily translatable to a specific reality. The suggestions will successively relate to academic education, scientific research and human relations management.

As far as *academic education* is concerned, we need to stress the importance of keeping in mind what it is all about: providing young people not only with skills and knowledge. Within genuine academic education, in order to enable the younger generation to take up important functions in society in their later career, we want to be democratic and provide fair chances to all. In this perspective it is imperative, and this is the first suggestion, that *all careers (except those that intrinsically imply a knowledge of a foreign language, such as language teaching) should be accessible on the basis of a domestic language study programme.* Universities should be compelled to provide such an offer themselves, in the case of larger comprehensive universities, or to provide it through interuniversity arrangements in at least one of the partner universities. Highly specialized academic education or university education tracks directed to an international audience, could be provided without domestic equivalent if this appears to be necessary. There are, however, two provisos in this context: highly specialized does also mean a very limited number of students; and addressing an international audience is a question of contents, not of recruitment policy.

Secondly, internationalisation of academic education also means a further stimulation of students to have a part of their *curriculum abroad* or to have at least some *international experience at home*. In this perspective, two remarks are necessary. Far too often the experience abroad is not really an experience in another country, but rather the experience of an international students' cocoon, following classes in English together, not seldom strictly separated from the domestic students. This is not entirely appropriate. An experience abroad should truly *immerse the student in the foreign country, its culture and language.* A serious effort in this direction needs to be made; the Erasmus programme had good intentions in this respect, but seems to have forgotten about them in practice.

The third suggestion in terms of academic education relates to linguistic diversity. Internationalisation requires more than one or two languages to be mastered. It simply is not enough that a university student masters their mother tongue and English (with a proficiency that is often of questionable quality). Especially in a multilingual country like Belgium, but also in other countries, the student should be exposed to a variety of foreign languages. Therefore, we can make a case for at least including a *third language* in any academic curriculum.

Let us now turn to *scientific research*. A first observation that needs to be made relates to the diversity between the various scientific research areas. The more 'exact' a science is, the bigger the influence of English becomes: natural sciences have the most, and humanities the least use of English. Therefore it is important to keep the policies at national and university level more general and allow room for discipline-specific adjustments. English is the *lingua franca* in many areas of science and while we may be happy with this or not, it is a fact. This fact should be taken as a starting point.

The first suggestion in terms of scientific research, then, would be to keep all scientific areas at least open for the use of other languages than English. This entails that any scientific community has the responsibility to *continue to develop the domestic scientific language*, even if the main research is totally or partially carried out in English. This means that e.g. European or national funding programmes would require not necessarily that the research applications are in a national language, but that the results and the main findings of research are also published in extensive domestic language publications. This is evident for dissemination of the findings, but should also be true for the research results as such. In case *funding is directly made dependent on complementary publication in the domestic language*, an important contribution to the development of the domestic language, and thus also to linguistic diversity may be expected. What is said for funding could also be repeated for taking into consideration peer reviewed publications.

The second suggestion related to research would be a general encouragement for scientists to deliver research results in the domestic language. This could be done by creating a *fund for the translation* of domestic publications into English or English-language publications into the domestic language. Publications of scientific research in the domestic language could also be stimulated by creating *awards or prizes* to honour people or publications which reflect the care for the development of domestic scientific language.

The third suggestion is related to what was mentioned at the start of the discussion of scientific research: not all areas of science are anglicized to the same extent. What is more, it may be less desirable to force a scientist to do research and publish for an international audience, as they should rather concentrate on domestic topics and ensure that their results are read by domestic policy makers. It is worrying to see that the research focus, in certain scientific areas, has so much shifted to international topics that whole areas that are only nationally relevant seem to be abandoned by scientific research. We can take the example of public health economics, highly relevant in all countries but very much connected to the domestic reality of hospitals, health care providers and national legislation. Examples could be multiplied: in nearly all sciences you have larger or smaller pockets of topics with high domestic relevance, but which are less attractive for the modern scientist who is pressured to publish on the fashionable international topics of the moment. It is difficult to stop this creation of scientific outcast areas, but it might be useful to create funding reserved for research in the domestic language or to reserve part of European, national or university research *funding for research in the domestic language on domestically highly relevant topics*, which are not sufficiently present on the international scientific stage.

Before we turn to our final observation of what we can do, the issue of *human resources* should be considered. Firstly, on many occasions internationalisation means that meetings will no longer be held in the domestic language as one or more participants do not master the language. The meeting is then held in English. This seems normal and natural, but probably restricts the ability of some others to fully engage in the discussions. This is often not sufficiently taken into consideration. *Meetings and documents with an official character*, which create new rules, new rights and duties, *should always be in the official, domestic language of the university*. This is a requirement of democratic participation of all and in line with the public language policy of the state. Translations may possibly be provided, but then translation into the international, not into the domestic language!

The second remark related to human resources is linked to the first: internationalisation will indeed often mean that universities recruit their researchers and professors internationally. The question arises whether we should oblige the *foreign recruited staff to know or learn the domestic official language* of the university. The answer is positive. This is self-evident when the recruited staff member is supposed to teach or do research in the domestic language, but also when he or she is only to teach in English and do research in this language. The basic knowledge of the domestic language will not only allow them to better interact with students and colleagues, but also to provide service to the local community, which at the end of the day most often funds their work. Moreover, can we really speak of an academic community, if some of its members cannot participate in the meetings, in the decision making or in the social life of the whole faculty and university? The pace at which and the degree to which a foreign colleague should master the domestic language is of course open for discussion; that this knowledge needs to be proven at a certain point in time is not.

The final observation towards what we can do also leads to an appeal for a different approach and more cooperation. After all, now it seems that people taking up the defence of their own linguistic identity do so very often in their own narrow national context. Proud national associations for the defence of the national language will refuse to use any other language, as they consider this contrary to their own high mission. This is fundamentally wrong. The defence of the French language in France and indeed Belgium, is also of my concern, as is the promotion of Danish in Denmark, or indeed the Dutch language in the Netherlands and Flanders. Making internationalisation and linguistic diversity go hand in hand, implies that *those concerned with the defence of their own language and culture find each other, talk to each other—if need be in English—in order to promote linguistic diversity.* At a European level, partners will have to be sought to influence the EU's involvement in teaching and research. The aim will be to change the current *de facto* dominance of English, and to move towards an approach that better realizes the 'unity in diversity' values that lie at the heart of the European Union. At an international level, partners will have to be sought to analyse—and as far as possible neutralize—the substantive impact of the dominance of English as a disciplinary language.

In our efforts for our own language, it should be only normal to bring together different people from a wide variety of countries to promote the national languages and identities, and in doing so we simultaneously demonstrate the power of international exchanges. This is yet another way of how internationalisation and the protection of the national language are inextricably bound together, and serve to make each other stronger.

Ten Policy Suggestions for Further Action

1. All universities have to guarantee that all careers (except those that intrinsically imply a knowledge of a foreign language, such as language teaching) are accessible on the basis of a domestic language study programme; each university will provide the corresponding educational tracks itself or through networks between universities.
2. All students should be required to spend part of their curriculum abroad or have an internationalisation at home experience.
3. The experience abroad should really immerse the student in the foreign country, its culture and language; not confine him/her to a ghetto of English-speaking foreign students.
4. Researchers have the duty to continuously develop the domestic scientific language; in order to stimulate them to do so, funding and acknowledgement of the research should be made dependent on publication of the research results in the domestic language (next to possible others).
5. A fund should be established to finance the translation of research in English into the domestic language and of domestic language research into English.
6. Prizes or awards should be created for those who have contributed most to the development of the domestic scientific language in their discipline.

7. Special funding should be reserved for research in the domestic language on domestically highly relevant topics that are not sufficiently present on the international scientific stage.
8. Meetings and documents which bear an official character, which create new rules, new rights and duties, should always be in the official, domestic language.
9. It is legitimate to expect that all recruited foreign staff knows or learns the official, domestic language of the university. The pace at which and the degree to which a foreign colleague should master the domestic language may vary; at a certain point in time, however, this knowledge needs to be present and proven.
10. Those concerned with the defense of their own language and culture need to find each other and network, if need be in English, in order to promote linguistic diversity.

Appendix

Table 1.5: PLI Results (Chinese and Hindustani Languages Merged)

RANK	SCORE	LANGUAGE	NATIVE (MIL)	GEO.	ECON.	COMM.	K&M	DIPL.
1	0.889	English	446.0	1	1	1	1	1
2	0.411	Mandarin	960.0	6	2	2	3	6
3	0.337	French	80.0	2	6	5	5	1
4	0.329	Spanish	470.0	3	5	3	7	3
5	0.273	Arabic	295.0	4	9	6	18	4
6	0.244	Russian	150.0	5	13	10	9	5
7	0.191	German	92.5	8	3	7	4	8
8	0.134	Hindi	376.0	10	12	8	2	10
9	0.133	Japanese	125.0	26	4	22	6	7
10	0.119	Portuguese	215.0	7	19	13	12	9
11	0.116	Cantonese	80.0	21	11	4	13	10
12	0.108	Italian	64.0	11	8	19	8	10
13	0.084	Dutch	22.0	16	7	24	11	10
14	0.077	Malay	77.0	9	17	21	22	10
15	0.055	Polish	40.0	23	22	23	15	10
16	0.053	Korean	80.0	22	15	37	10	10
17	0.047	Turkish	75.0	12	24	38	16	10
18	0.046	Romanian	24.0	25	37	20	41	10
19	0.043	Norwegian	5.0	42	10	106	25	10
20	0.041	Swedish	9.2	35	14	72	14	10
21	0.040	Persian	52.5	14	36	30	17	10
22	0.034	Danish	5.5	41	16	84	20	10
23	0.034	Hebrew	4.4	57	23	36	21	10
24	0.033	Czech	10.6	36	21	45	27	10
25	0.033	Kazakh	11.0	15	32	57	55	10
26	0.032	Thai	56.0	17	33	65	37	10
27	0.032	Finnish	5.4	45	18	90	19	10
28	0.032	Ukrainian	30.0	18	49	27	58	10
29	0.030	Tamil	70.0	34	34	31	56	10
30	0.029	Bengali	210.0	70	73	26	36	10
31	0.029	Greek	13.0	20	28	89	24	10
32	0.028	Serbo-Croatian	19.0	19	44	47	47	10
33	0.028	Slovak	5.2	47	26	53	48	10

(*continued on next page*)

Table 1.5: (continued)

RANK	SCORE	LANGUAGE	NATIVE (MIL)	GEO.	ECON.	COMM.	K&M	DIPL.
34	0.027	Slovene	2.5	63	27	52	40	10
35	0.027	Maltese	0.5	71	25	48	64	10
36	0.026	Hungarian	13.0	32	30	71	38	10
37	0.026	Swahili	10.0	13	78	59	69	10
38	0.026	Javanese	82.0	30	40	32	69	10
39	0.024	Icelandic	0.3	69	20	119	52	10
40	0.023	Bulgarian	9.0	43	39	49	44	10
41	0.023	Latvian	7.8	66	35	54	57	10
42	0.020	Belarusian	7.6	65	38	56	64	10
43	0.019	Vietnamese	76.0	33	48	70	23	10
44	0.019	Azerbaijani	26.0	60	41	64	49	10
45	0.019	Punjabi	100.0	37	59	41	69	10
46	0.019	Tagalog	28.0	44	52	61	26	10
47	0.017	Estonian	1.2	56	31	120	50	10
48	0.017	Lithuanian	3.0	61	29	117	59	10
49	0.017	Turkmen	8.0	51	42	76	69	10
50	0.016	Zulu	12.0	39	45	79	45	10
51	0.016	Macedonian	2.0	76	47	60	62	10
52	0.015	Xhosa	8.2	39	45	94	45	10
53	0.015	Pashto	50.0	27	72	69	69	10
54	0.014	Sindhi	75.0	62	69	50	69	10
55	0.014	Amharic	25.0	54	96	42	69	10
56	0.014	Uyghur	10.4	29	67	75	69	10
57	0.013	Tigrinya	6.9	72	115	46	39	10
58	0.013	Mongolian	10.0	24	51	116	52	10
59	0.013	Odia	33.0	89	94	34	69	10
60	0.013	Uzbek	27.0	46	71	68	69	10
61	0.013	Bhojpuri	40.0	103	95	33	69	10
62	0.012	Telugu	76.0	82	91	43	69	10
63	0.012	Maithili	30.0	103	109	35	69	10
64	0.012	Sinhalese	16.0	68	50	78	69	10
65	0.012	Assamese	15.0	92	98	39	69	10
66	0.011	Magahi	14.0	103	109	40	69	10
67	0.011	Malagasy	18.0	48	114	62	69	10
68	0.011	Sylheti	11.0	97	116	44	69	10
69	0.011	Burmese	33.0	38	74	87	43	10

Table 1.5: (continued)

RANK	SCORE	LANGUAGE	NATIVE (MIL)	GEO.	ECON.	COMM.	K&M	DIPL.
70	0.011	Sundanese	38.0	93	77	55	69	10
71	0.010	Kannada	38.1	86	92	51	69	10
72	0.010	Kyrgyz	4.3	52	85	73	64	10
73	0.009	Georgian	4.3	50	56	110	51	10
74	0.009	Malayalam	38.0	96	97	58	69	10
75	0.009	Madurese	15.0	100	84	63	69	10
76	0.009	Marathi	73.0	81	90	66	69	10
77	0.009	Lao	3.3	53	75	88	63	10
78	0.009	Kurdish	25.0	91	68	74	69	10
79	0.008	Zhuang	16.0	103	53	92	69	10
80	0.007	Somali	17.0	31	121	97	69	10
81	0.007	Saraiki	20.0	103	109	67	69	10
82	0.007	Bambara	4.0	28	106	112	64	10
83	0.007	Armenian	10.0	73	61	111	60	10
84	0.007	Khmer	16.0	49	80	108	52	10
85	0.007	Balochi	7.6	103	76	80	69	10
86	0.007	Quechua	8.9	55	70	115	69	10
87	0.006	Gujarati	50.0	85	93	77	69	10
88	0.006	Bhutanese	0.2	77	66	124	42	10
89	0.006	Fijian	0.3	75	60	123	64	10
90	0.006	Nepali	25.0	64	88	99	69	10
91	0.005	Marwari	22.0	103	81	85	69	10
92	0.005	Dakhini	11.0	83	104	82	69	10
93	0.005	Chewa	12.0	67	117	101	69	10
94	0.005	Cebuano	21.0	98	79	91	69	10
95	0.005	Hmong	8.4	103	62	121	69	10
96	0.005	Wolof	4.2	59	89	113	60	10
97	0.005	Kinyarwanda	9.8	74	105	102	69	10
98	0.004	Yoruba	28.0	103	86	93	69	10
99	0.004	Konkani	7.4	101	108	86	69	10
100	0.004	Igbo	25.0	103	86	96	69	10
101	0.004	Ilocano	9.1	103	81	98	69	10
102	0.004	Hiligaynon	8.2	103	81	100	69	10
103	0.004	Hausa	34.0	103	123	81	69	10
104	0.004	Kirundi	8.8	79	120	103	69	10

(*continued on next page*)

Table 1.5: (continued)

RANK	SCORE	LANGUAGE	NATIVE (MIL)	GEO.	ECON.	COMM.	K&M	DIPL.
105	0.004	Oromo	38.0	103	122	83	69	10
106	0.004	Dhundhari	9.6	95	109	95	69	10
107	0.004	Mossi	7.6	58	103	122	69	10
108	0.004	Fula	24.0	80	118	105	69	10
109	0.003	Haitian Creole	9.6	78	102	118	69	10
110	0.003	Haryanvi	14.0	94	100	109	69	10
111	0.003	Shona	8.3	103	119	104	69	10
112	0.002	Chittagonian	16.0	102	107	107	69	10
113	0.002	Akan	11.0	103	101	114	69	10

DUISBURGER ARBEITEN ZUR SPRACH- UND KULTURWISSENSCHAFT
DUISBURG PAPERS ON RESEARCH IN LANGUAGE AND CULTURE

Herausgegeben von / edited by Frank Polzenhagen und / and Monika Reif
Begründet von / founded by Ulrich Ammon, René Dirven und / and Martin Pütz

Die Titel bis Band 89 finden Sie unter www.peterlang.com/view/serial/DASK
See www.peterlang.com/view/serial/DASK for volumes 1 - 89.

Band 90 Maria-Antonia Kontostathi: Die Arbeit mit dem Europäischen Sprachenportfolio als Möglichkeit zum selbständigen Erarbeiten fremdsprachlicher Kompetenzen. 2012.

Band 91 Yu Chen: Verbessern chinesische Studierende ihre Sprechfertigkeit im Deutschen während des Fachstudiums in Deutschland? Eine empirische Untersuchung unter Berücksichtigung sozialer Aspekte. 2012.

Band 92 Jakob Haselhuber: Mehrsprachigkeit in der Europäischen Union. Eine Analyse der EU-Sprachenpolitik, mit besonderem Fokus auf Deutschland. Umfassende Dokumentation und Perspektiven für die Zukunft. 2012.

Band 93 Hans Wagener: Untergräbt Deutschland selbst die internationale Stellung der deutschen Sprache? Eine Folge der Förderung von Englisch im Bildungsbereich. 2012.

Band 94 G. Stickel / M. Carrier (eds.) · Language Education in Creating a Multilingual Europe. Contributions to the Annual Conference 2011 of EFNIL in London. 2012.

Band 95 Jun He: Die Auswirkungen der englischsprachigen Hochschullehre in Deutschland auf das Deutschlernen in China. 2013.

Band 96 Monika Reif / Justyna A. Robinson / Martin Pütz (eds.): Variation in Language and Language Use. Linguistic, Socio-Cultural and Cognitive Perspectives. 2013.

Band 97 Carla Figueira: Languages at War. External Language Spread Policies in Lusophone Africa. Mozambique and Guinea-Bissau at the Turn of the 21st Century. 2013.

Band 98 Siew Imm Tan: Malaysian English. Language Contact and Change. 2013.

Band 99 Gerhard Stickel / Tamás Váradi (eds.): Lexical Challenges in a Multilingual Europe. Contributions to the Annual Conference 2012 of EFNIL in Budapest. 2013.

Band 100 Liudmila Li: Die Problematik der sprachlichen Integration von ImmigrantInnen. Unter Berücksichtigung des staatlich geforderten Sprachniveaus B1 (GER). Verbesserungsvorschläge auf Grundlage der empirischen Untersuchung in Berlin-Moabit. 2014.

Band 101 Xiaoyan Xia: Categorization and L2 Vocabulary Learning. A Cognitive Linguistic Perspective. 2014.

Band 102 Gerhard Stickel (ed.): Translation and Interpretation in Europe. Contributions to the Annual Conference 2013 of EFNIL in Vilnius. 2014.

Band 103 Maciej Mackiewicz: Interkulturelle Motivation im Fremdsprachenunterricht. Eine komparative Studie zu Deutsch als Fremdsprache in Polen und den USA. 2014.

Band 104 Silke Gester / Erika Kegyes (Hrsg.): Quo vadis, DaF? II. Betrachtungen zu Deutsch als Fremdsprache in den Ländern der Visegrád-Gruppe. 2015.

Band 105 Miroslava Majtanova: Die Rolle der deutschen Sprache für die Gruppenidentität von Deutschen im Ausland. Am Beispiel des Vereinslebens in Kuala Lumpur. 2015.

Band 106 Julia Wesian: Danksagungen in Dissertationen. Zur Genese einer Textsorte. 2015.

Band 107 Hector Kamdem Fonkoua: A Dictionary of Camfranglais. 2015.

Band 108 Frauke Priegnitz: Zwischen englischsprachigem Studium und landessprachigem Umfeld. Internationale Absolventen deutscher und dänischer Hochschulen. 2015.

Band 109 Gerhard Stickel / Cecilia Robustelli (eds.): Language Use in University Teaching and Research. Contributions to the Annual Conference 2014 of EFNIL in Florence. 2015.

Band 110 Wenting Sheng: Sprachförderungspolitik Deutschlands, Großbritanniens und Chinas im Vergleich. 2015.

Band 111 Eglė Kontutytė / Vaiva Žeimantienė (Hrsg.): Sprache in der Wissenschaft. Germanistische Einblicke. 2016.

Band 112 Ludmila Zemková: The Use of Gender Markers in Animals. As Demonstrated by Issues of National Geographic. 2015.

Band 113 Oromiya-Jalata Deffa: Discursive Construction of Bicultural Identity. A Cross-Generational Sociolinguistic Study on Oromo-Americans in Minnesota. 2016.

Band 114 Martin Pütz / Neele Mundt (eds.): Vanishing Languages in Context. Ideological, Attitudinal and Social Identity Perspectives. 2016.

Band 115 Julia Schultz: Twentieth Century Borrowings from German to English. Their Semantic Integration and Contextual Usage. 2016.

Band 116 Arne Peters: Linguistic Change in Galway City English. A Variationist Sociolinguistic Study of (th) and (dh) in Urban Western Irish English. 2016.

Band 117 Elena Maria Pandolfi / Johanna Miecznikowski / Sabine Christopher / Alain Kamber (eds.): Studies on Language Norms in Context. 2017.

Band 118 Shenwei Zhang: Nationale und regionale Standardvarianten des Deutschen im Unterricht von Deutsch als Fremdsprache für Chinesen. 2017.

Band 119 Lillian Brise: 'Eating Regret and Seeing Contempt' - A Cognitive Linguistic Approach to the Language of Emotions in Igala (Nigeria). 2017.

Band 120 Sandro M. Moraldo (Hrsg.): Die deutsche Sprache in Italien – Zwischen Europäisierung und Globalisierung. 2017.

Band 121 Abdulhamid Abdulrahman: Tiermetaphorik in unterschiedlichen Diskurstraditionen. 2018.

Band 122 Patrizia Danuta Kleebauer: Multilingualismus erwachsener Migrantinnen und Migranten polnischer Herkunft. Eine qualitative Untersuchung in Deutschland und Schweden. 2018

Band 123 Stefanie Vogelbacher: Scenario Negotiation in Online Debates about the European Union. Analysing Metaphor in Communication. 2019.

Band 124 Helene Steigertahl: English(es) in Post-Independence Namibia. An Investigation of Variety Status and Its Implications for English Language Teaching. 2020.

Band 125 Anke Beger: The Role of (Deliberate) Metaphor in Communicating Knowledge in Academic Discourse - An Analysis of College Lectures from Different Disciplines. 2019.

Band 126 Danny Pieters / Thijs Keersmaekers (eds.): Internationalisation of Universities and the National Language - Language Policy Interventions and Case Studies. 2020.

www.peterlang.com

www.ingramcontent.com/pod-product-compliance
Ingram Content Group UK Ltd.
Pitfield, Milton Keynes, MK11 3LW, UK
UKHW041829100926
8556IPUK00002B/82

9 783631 816868